FEAR COMPUTERS NO MORE

Danny Goodman

with

Katherine Murray

Fear Computers No More

Danny Goodman
with
Katherine Murray

///|Brady

New York   London   Toronto   Sydney   Tokyo   Singapore

Brady Publishing

A Division of Prentice Hall Computer Publishing
15 Columbus Circle
New York, NY 10023

ISBN: 1-56686-086-5
Library of Congress Catalog No.: 93-25267

Printing Code: The rightmost double-digit number is the year of the book's printing; the rightmost single-digit number is the number of the book's printing. For example, 93-1 shows that the first printing of the book occurred in 1993.

96 95 94 93   4 3 2 1

Manufactured in the United States of America

Dedication

To Cameron, who spent the first month of his life in Mom's office while she wrote this book.

About the Author

(Written by 5-year-old Christopher Murray)

My mom's name is Kathy Murray (but I call her Mommy). She's 1475 years old, has brown hair, and is as tall as her computer. Sometimes, when she makes a face, she looks like Captain Hook. She makes money by typing on a keyboard, and the guy comes and brings her packages every day. (*Mom's Note:* That's the Federal Express guy, don't call Miami Vice!) She likes to play Legos with me and watch the *Dick Van Dyke Show*, and she's the best mom I ever had.

Acknowledgments

Gremlin-battling is an exhausting process. Special thanks to the exterminating efforts of the following people:

Kelly (KiDDo) Dobbs, managing editor of Brady, for her laser-point focus (capable of burning out typos at a single glance), her brilliant wit (able to leap tall mensas in a single bound), and her unrecordable pace (faster than a speeding Concord).

Jono Hardjowirogo, Brady acquisitions director, for raising an eyebrow and wondering about me in the first place.

Danny Goodman, series author, for his vision and thoughtful creation of this series. Thanks for letting me help.

John Gieg, the Creature Guy, for creating perfect little monsters that are tamed in the pages of this book. (Someone should nominate him for best computer book illustrator of the year. Does anyone second the motion?)

My agent, Claudette Moore of Moore Literary Agency, who does the hard stuff (legal junk) so that I can do the fun stuff (write).

My family—nuclear and extended—who, as always, put up with a mom that rushes from the computer to the kitchen to the nursery and back to the computer, sometimes with a phone on one shoulder and a baby on the other. You guys are racking up some good Karma by putting up with me.

Credits

Publisher
Michael Violano

Acquisitions Director
Jono Hardjowirogo

Managing Editor
Kelly D. Dobbs

Editorial Assistant
Lisa Rose

Illustrator
John Leonard Gieg

Book Designer
Michele Laseau, Kevin Spear

Cover Designer
Jay Corpus

Indexer
Craig Small, Caroline Roop

Production Team
Diana Bigham, Katy Bodenmiller, Scott Cook, Tim Cox,
Mark Enochs, Linda Koopman, Tom Loveman, Beth Rago,
Carrie Roth, Greg Simsic

Marketing Director
Lonny Stein

Marketing Coordinator
Laura Cadorette

Contents

Introduction

Maybe you were kidding yourself, but you thought this day would never come. You watched while your coworkers, friends, and neighbors—one by one—jumped on the computer bandwagon. That's not for *me*, you said as they gathered in groups to toss about pieces of computer jargon and impress each other with their new-found knowledge. That stuff about CPUs, hard disk capacity, high-resolution displays, and laser printers went right over your head. And good riddance. Your hands-on method of running your office works just fine, thank you very much. The One-Write system of accounting, the Smith-Corona method of writing letters, and the good ol' filing cabinet strategy for data management suits you like a favorite pair of warm pajamas.

But things change.

One day you walk into your office and a cold-and-sterile-looking (and not to mention unfriendly) computer glares at you from your very own desktop. You didn't ask for it. You didn't want it. But somebody higher up decided that you needed it. Someone, somewhere, did a study of Things As They Are and came to the conclusion that your work will somehow be enhanced, that you'll be more productive, that the entire organization will somehow benefit from fixing a system that isn't broken.

Now the choice is no longer yours—you've already lost your position as one of the strongholds for the Good Old Days. Your arguments for the hands-on methods so familiar to you have been swept away with the acquisition of a single machine. No use crying over bought equipment; now it's up to you to make the best of the situation.

That's precisely what *Fear Computers No More* is here to help you do. We know that you're not thrilled with the prospect of learning what all this computer hoopla is about. We understand that you're using a computer—or perhaps purchasing one—only because you can no longer avoid it. For whatever reason—whether the kids have surpassed your understanding of technology, the boss insists, or your business needs a shot in the arm—you find yourself in a position of needing to get past your computer bias and, sooner rather than later, get things done.

Confronting Your Fears

You may not want to admit it—most people don't—but the single biggest stumbling block in your way as you begin to work with computers is intimidation. Sure, it's a small metal box. Yeah, you slide those square things in, and they store something vaguely referred to as "data." Seems harmless enough. But there's something bigger that worries you, something that makes learning enough about your computer to use it productively seem like an insurmountable task.

That something is fear. And it comes in five flavors:

- Fear of messing up.
- Fear of looking stupid.
- Fear of the unknown.
- Fear of change.
- Fear of fear.

You know the fear of messing up: we've all felt it. Whether it's a big one or a small one, those screw-ups scream "Amateur!" People peek over cubicle walls when they hear your computer beeping frantically at you. Managers come out of their offices; secretaries pause momentarily on the phone; coworkers hush their conversations. What if you do something really awful and become an office anecdote? Then people gather by the coffee maker to discuss your latest faux pas.

That leads right into looking stupid, doesn't it? Chances are, if coworkers are discussing you over Maxwell House and yeast donuts, you've branded yourself—at least for a while. But even in a milder case, when no one particularly notices the mistake, we hate to look any less than competent. We don't want to struggle with learning curves because, while we're at the bottom, we tend to *look* like we're at the bottom. Things get more comfortable as we edge up toward the top of the curve—then it's okay to tell people "I'm just learning."

Fear of the unknown is a big one. When the computer starts beeping, will it ever stop? What if you do something and blow away an important program? What if you just can't get the hang of the word processing program everyone else uses? Until you sit down and actually start using the machine, the fear of what might happen takes on a life of its own.

Not too many people are thrilled with the prospect of change, whether you're talking about changing vehicles or changing jobs. Change means things will be different, that we will no longer know what to expect. Change means that we have to get used to something new, and even though the something we've got may not be working real well, hey, at least we're used to it. Change means that we have to stretch our boundaries a bit and try things we haven't tried before. Pretty scary.

The last one—the fear of fear—is the little gremlin that paints a picture in your brain of you, six months from now, still as panicked as you are today. What if you use this thing, day-in and day-out, and, after a considerable length of time, you are still as beset with worries as you are now? What if people get tired of bailing you out; the tech support people won't answer your calls; and even your best friend advises you to "Give up the computer literacy stuff?"

Take a deep breath and relax. Then invite all those little fear monsters to come on out and have a cup of coffee. Through the course of this book, you'll learn that those little devils that seem so scary now are no more than figments of your imagination.

What You'll Find in *Fear Computers No More*

In this book, you'll find a unique approach to dealing with your computer intimidation. The best weapon against fear in any form is education—and we've packed all the basics between the covers of this book. Specifically, you'll find that the following elements come together to make learning about computers nonthreatening and perhaps (dare we say it?) fun:

- A set of 20 encounters, each helping you to learn a new computer skill and to dispel a demon

- Goal statements clearly defining what you will accomplish in each session

- What-You-Will-Need sections that tell you, up front, the elements you need for each successful encounter

- Terms of Enfearment, which highlight the computer buzz words you'll master in each encounter

- Briefings, in which the main explanation of the encounter takes place, showing Things As They Should Be

- They're Out To Get Us sections detailing what might happen when Things *Aren't* As They Should Be

- Demon-strations, which allow you to practice hands-on examples of each encounter's topic

- Summaries, which give you a broadbrush overview of the topics introduced

- Exorcises, sets of fill-in-the-blank and multiple-choice questions that allow you to test what you've learned and to make sure that you've rid yourself of that particular encounter's gremlin.

Throughout the book, you'll see screen shots when you need them and illustrations of those buggy little monsters pop up all over the place. Tables are also used, as needed, to highlight information in columnar format. Additionally, you'll find numbered steps and bulleted lists in passages where extra emphasis is given to steps in a tutorial section or to items in a series.

All in all, you should find all the education and the reinforcement you need in *Fear Computers No More*. With a format that enables you to master just what you need and to move on, you won't get bogged down in lengthy explanations and impractical examples. *Fear Computers No More* will help you move from the world of Computer Dread to the ranks of Computer Users.

What You *Won't* Find in *Fear Computers No More*

The best books don't try to be all things to all people. In *Fear Computers No More*, there are many things you won't see:

- You won't find explanations of super-technical procedures.

- There will be no tips for high-end users.

- You will not build a sophisticated spreadsheet.

- You won't use macros, programming languages, or gimicky batch files.

- You won't be assaulted with computer jargon.

- You will not find lengthy explanations about esoteric features you'll never use.

In a bold attempt to give you only what you need to slay your computer dragons and to get on the road to computer productivity, *Fear Computers No More* helps you learn the basics—just what you need to get going—and then gets out of your way. No unnecessary hand-holding, verbose descriptions, or long-winded fictional examples.

Who's Afraid of a Little Computer?

Most of us need a little shove as we teeter on the brink of computerization. Why learn something new if we don't have to? The learning curve is staggering, and the fact that most of our friends and coworkers have been using computers for years doesn't help us any. Specifically, *Fear Computers No More* speaks to the following readers:

- Readers who are begrudgingly thinking about purchasing a computer but don't know where to start

- People who have recently been introduced to computers at work

- Support personnel who have inherited a system they now need to figure out

- Anyone who wants to understand the basics of using a computer but has no desire to become a computer expert

Whether your computer needs are small or large, whether the number of gremlins that plague you are few or many, *Fear Computers No More* will help you take those first shaky steps into the realm of computerization.

Now, if you're ready, think a Happy Thought, and follow me. . .

What a Computer Can— and Can't—Do

Goal

To find out how a computer can help you in your daily—or not so daily—tasks.

What You Will Need

Only a mildly inquisitive nature (as far as computers are concerned).

Terms of Enfearment

mainframe	compatibles
personal computer	software
Apple computers	Macintosh
IBM PC	

Briefing

So we've established that—like it or not—you are facing the prospect of using and perhaps purchasing a computer for the first time. Granted, you're coming into the computer industry as Rip Van Winkle—you've been sleeping for two decades while the rest of the industry evolved without you. As you begin to learn about the machines that you've avoided for so long, there's no need to become a computer expert (that mythological creature); all you want to do is learn enough to get a few things done (or perhaps just enough to please your boss) and get on with the important things in your life. But, by the same token, a little background information can't hurt.

Where Did Computers Come From, Anyway?

Before the first personal computer occupied a desktop, computers were room-sized, sophisticated pieces of equipment, used only by people in white coats with computer-science degrees. These huge computers—known as *mainframes*—ran corporations, stored data, and performed a myriad of complex operations that were lost on the general public. Mainframes, and their smaller counterparts, *minicomputers,* are still used today all across the world. Their number is far outdistanced by their smaller and more personal cousins.

A smaller computer that could be used by everyday people was a gleam in more than one hobbyist's eye. They toyed with the idea of having a small system, one that ran programs, played games, and stored information on a small scale. The first real "personal" computer was the product of some late-night brainstorming and garage tinkering by Steve Jobs and Steve Wozniak, developers of the *Apple I* (see fig. 1.1). The Apple was computing power—though only a small amount of it—in a small case. Hardly more than a toy, the Apple I lit a fire in the imagination of computer hobbyists everywhere. Even though the Apple did almost nothing by today's standards, the potential was there.

Figure 1.1
A little of this, a little of that, and voila! A computer.

The evolutionary Apple I grew into the Apple II, and the computer age began its many-year shift into high gear. The Apple II spread like wildfire in schools, introducing computer literacy to an entire generation before their parents had a chance to find out what the fuss was about.

Soon after the success of the Apple II became apparent, IBM struck out into the market with its first shot at a personal computer: the IBM PC. The reception of the IBM PC was not lost on IBM's competitors; soon other companies like Atari and Radio Shack were introducing their own new computer systems.

Even while the enthusiasm for personal computing was snowballing, a general wave of discontentment began spreading through the eclectic PC community. Sure, these things were cool to play with. Yes, we can do a few things on our desktops we couldn't do before. But why is the blasted thing so difficult to use?

Even though the computers themselves were working the way hobbyists had envisioned them, the people creating the software (the programs that we use on the computer) weren't making things easy. The programs smacked of the genius of those white-coated computer-science majors; we ordinary folk found the programs to be cumbersome and complicated for no apparent reason.

One important program, the operating system of the early PCs, was a real turn-off for people trying computing for the first time. In order to do anything with DOS, users had to enter cryptic commands on a cold, un-friendly command line (see fig. 1.2). Remembering the commands was hard enough, but trying not to do the things DOS got fussy over (using spaces in command lines, including more than eight characters in a filename, etc.) made the whole DOS experience intimidating for people who found them-selves toward the beginning end of the learning curve.

Figure 1.2
Abandoned and alone at the cold DOS prompt.

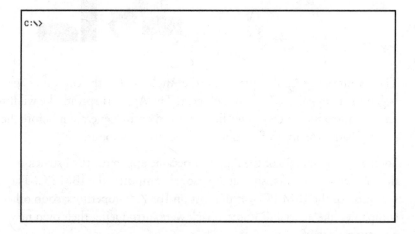

```
c:\>
```

If you feel a DOS-knot tightening in your stomach as you think about working with the operating system on your new PC, you may be experiencing a DOS flashback. Even if you didn't use computers during that age of evolution, chances are that you've heard the DOS horror stories of your friends and coworkers. Here's a news flash: The makers of DOS saw the light quite a while ago, creating subsequent versions (we're up to Version 6.0 now) that were friendlier and gave the user the option of bypassing that scary command line. For more about operating systems and DOS, see the 17th Encounter.

A new computer arrived in 1984, showing us that a friendlier alternative was possible. The *Macintosh*, produced by Apple as "the computer for the rest of us" allowed users to open files, work with programs, and perform many tasks by using pictures on the screen (see fig. 1.3). The Mac was the first system to introduce the mouse, a small hand-held device that you use to select items on-screen. The whole machine was created to be easy to use—something that hadn't yet occurred to the PC side of personal computing.

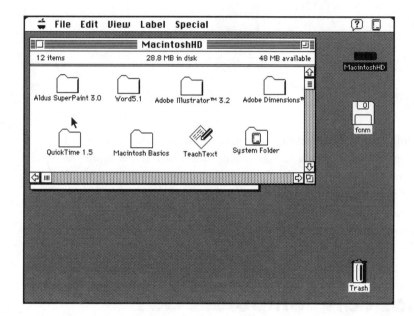

Figure 1.3
The Macintosh brought new life to the screen in the form of pictures that were easy to understand.

Another major addition to the PC world was that of competition: soon after IBM made a big splash with the IBM PC, manufacturers all over the world were rushing to the market with their own PC lookalikes. These computers, known as *IBM-compatibles* or *clones*, looked (somewhat) like IBMs, quacked like IBMs, but weren't true IBMs. The clones were able to offer to users personal computing power at a fraction of the cost inflated by the pricey IBM brand name.

Today, you'll find very definite PC camps and Macintosh camps. PC lovers often dislike the Macintosh and vice versa. Groupies from each arena are quick to defend the superlative powers of their chosen system (see fig. 1.4).

The truth is that both types of computer systems have evolved at a staggering rate, getting more powerful, faster, and smaller but with greater capacity for crunching more and more data. And we've seen the introduction of almost every add-on piece available (printers, monitors, modems, scanners, mice, faxes), each with its own evolution track.

Figure 1.4
Which computer is best? Yours, of course.

Thankfully, the programs we use on our computers have also changed for the better. Although programs continued, for a while, to get more and more complicated, most software developers today recognize that in order for a program to be successful, people have to want to use it. And people don't want to use programs that are confusing, unfriendly, and frustrating. We want things simple, so we can do what we need to do with our computers and then get on with our lives.

What Can Computers Do?

You may not be in much of a mood to hear it, but it's true: Computers *can* make your life easier. Your work life, at least. After you wrestle your fears into submission, you'll begin to discover that the computer really can help you get some things done more quickly, some things more accurately, and some things more completely. Almost against your will, you will see sooner or later that there are benefits to these annoying things with their continually blinking cursors and error-shrieking beeps.

Specifically, what your computer can do—that is, the type of programs you run and the day-in, day-out tasks you use your computer to perform—will depend on several factors: the computer you purchase (or are assigned), the programs you get to run on the computer, and the extra items you use with the system (for example, you can't run telecommunications software if you don't have a modem).

Here's a quick look at a few of the good things that may come of your computer experience:

■ **Your computer can automate repetitive tasks.** Suppose that it's part of your job to write follow-up correspondence for all sales managers in your region. You take the time to organize all the addresses of new clients, then type the letters and envelopes, and mail the letters out. If you type each letter by itself, you spend quite a bit of your day typing the same things over and over. If you use a carbon and type three or four copies at a time, you lessen the number of times you type the letter, but the clients will know they were carboned (not a real professional look). You could have the form letter professionally copied and then type in the names of the individual clients, but once again, the clients will be on to your little time-saving ploy. The answer? A computer with a word processing program, preferably with a mail-merge utility (a program that keeps track of names and addresses so that you can add them to your letters easily). You can type and save the letter and have the program add the necessary names as the letters are printed (see fig. 1.5). Now you can go get a well-deserved cup of coffee while the computer does the rest.

■ **The programs you use can enhance the accuracy of your work.** If you're not a numbers person, you'll find yourself happily relying on the fool-safe processing your computer offers you. Never again do you have to balance that checkbook by hand, figure payroll, or guess on taxes. And the accuracy-checking is available for text; many programs have built-in utilities that check your grammar, rate your overall writing style, and double-check your spelling (see fig. 1.6).

Figure 1.5
*Let your computer do
those boring routine
tasks.*

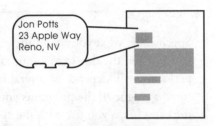

Figure 1.6
*Your computer can
weed out those typos.*

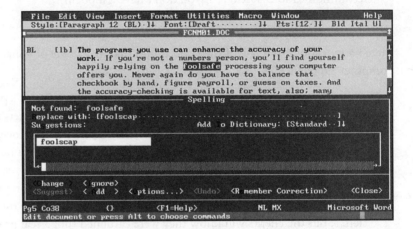

■ **You'll be able to create professional-looking products by yourself.**
Just a few years ago, producing a corporate report involved a dozen
people—writers, editors, typesetters, layout people, proofreaders, and
printers. If your company didn't have all those people on staff, you had
to go to an outside agency to get all the bases covered—an oftentimes
enormous cost in terms of time and money. Today, our personal
computers can become publishing systems. You can replace all those
people yourself and produce that report in a fraction of the time you
used to spend waiting on the finished product. Most popular programs
today give you the option of high-quality printing, producing output
that is a close second to professionally done documents.

■ **Your computer can help you lighten your workload.** It may seem
improbable now, but after you learn the basics of using your computer,
you'll find dozens of ways it can make your job easier. You can look up
information right at your desktop instead of venturing out to the

public library. You can combine sections of text from your quarterly reports to create the annual report; the data is already there, ready to be used (see fig. 1.7). Calculations are a breeze. Project planning is a snap. Presentations are something miraculously close to fun. Because the computer lets you enter data—text, numbers, whatever—once and save it forever, you never have to repeat your work. This frees up time you previously spent doing grunt work (but it may also give your boss an excuse to heap more papers in your In basket).

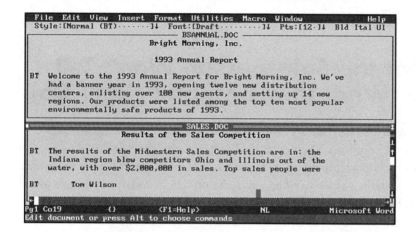

Figure 1.7
A little bit here, a little bit there, and you've got a report.

■ **The system will save you money (in the long run).** Experts can tell you precisely when your computer begins saving you money. Chances are, this point does not come about in the first few weeks, as you are struggling with your hardware and software and trying to find your way around. At some point, however, the computer becomes worth its investment. You're saving money by cutting out the outside services you previously relied on (typesetting, design, layout, bookkeeping, etc.). You may also be able to compete in different markets by providing a higher quality product. You can use your computer to do your taxes, manage your finances, and plan your investments.

■ **The connections you make can widen your horizons.** Even though the typical personal computer is a single, stand-alone system, PCs don't have to exist in a vaccuum. If you have a modem and a phone jack, you can join the ranks of millions of computer owners who link up, through the phone lines, to other computerists. You might want to join an information service (like CompuServe or GEnie), subscribe to E-mail (a message service you can access through your computer), or hook up to a bulletin board service that introduces you to other computer users. You can even link up to the White House and leave some on-line messages for President Bill. Communication services can take you all over the world—literally—and let you investigate any number of topics that interest you. (For more about modems, see the 14th Encounter.)

What the Salesperson Won't Tell You (What the Computer Can't Do)

Oh, sure, that salesperson seems helpful enough. He rattles on about the speed of the computer; shows you the literature with the 8-by-10 glossy photos of the sparkling monitors with razor-sharp clarity. He seems to think that this system—which just happens to be on special today—is the machine for you. But because he's thinking "commission, commission," he's not going to tell you a few other things you really should know:

- **The computer is not going to think for you.** Most computers—unless they are special package deals—are sold with no extra software (except, perhaps, the operating system). You won't be able to do anything right away unless you get the programs you need, which could run from a few hundred to a few thousand extra dollars. Ask the salesperson, "Does this computer come with any software?" and if he says yes, ask to see the software demonstrated. (You also may want to shop around to see who offers you the best package deal.)

- **The computer won't explain itself.** Although the Mac is pretty good about helping new users find their way around, most PCs aren't nearly as friendly as the new user would like (the exception being, perhaps, the PS/1). Take the initiative and read (or at least look through) the manuals that come with your system and allow yourself some start-up time with no deadline pressure so that you can figure out some of the computer basics before you get in a time crunch.

■ **"Any" computer isn't good enough.** Don't spend your time and money on a system that doesn't have all the features you need (see fig. 1.8). It may have a snazzy screen and a cool keyboard, but is the hard disk large enough? Do you need a CD-ROM drive? Does it have a modem? Educate yourself about your computer needs before you buy. It could save you from being sorry later. (See the 2nd Encounter to find out about your computer needs.)

Poor monitor?
Buy a new one--
pay $600.

Not enough memory?
Get an upgrade for
$300.

Hate the
keyboard? A
new one runs
you $120.

Dinky hard disk?
Write the check:
$350.

Figure 1.8
A bargain computer may not be such a bargain.

■ **Not all computers can "grow" with you.** Suppose that you really start getting into this computer thing and you want to add a printer, mouse, modem, and perhaps other toys like a graphics tablet. Does your computer have enough room inside to support all these items? (Add-ons are attached to your system through connectors called ports in the back of your computer. If you don't have the room, you can't add on.) When you're thinking about purchasing a system, make sure that the computer you choose will be able to grow with you in the future.

■ **Computers aren't compatible with everything.** A friend recently purchased a computer for her kids. Excitedly, she went out and bought an armload of programs—things with neat pictures on the cover, like Mickey Mouse and the Cookie Monster. She didn't notice the stickers on the bottom of the boxes, the ones that said IBM PC or Apple II. One said Commodore. What did she have? A bunch of programs that didn't work on her computer. Remember that certain computers use certain types of programs. If you use a PC, make sure that you get programs that run on a PC. If you use the Mac, look for Mac programs. If you can't tell from the outside of the box what type of computer runs the program you're considering, ask someone.

Compatibility is becoming less of an issue today, thanks to a special add-in board that allows the Macintosh to work with files you create on a PC. For more information, see the 17th Encounter.

They're Out To Get Us

Perhaps the biggest problem you will face, if you are trying to make an educated decision, is which computer to buy. Computer manufacturers don't make this any easier by glutting the market with a million and one different computers with two million different variations. As if the individual differences weren't enough, there are tower systems, desktop systems, notebooks, laptops, and palmtops (this list goes on and on). For more about computer differences, see the 3rd Encounter.

Don't feel like you need to analyze everything before you buy. That would take several months, full-time, and by then everything would be outdated anyway. Keep these tips in mind as you try to get a grasp on the kind of system you are looking for:

■ Don't feel like you need to get on-the-edge technology. Most new technology includes a few bugs that need to be worked out, so you'll benefit by waiting until the system ages a bit before you invest.

■ Remember that the ads are trying to sell you something (don't believe everything you read). Do your own investigating—whether you're thinking of buying a new computer or a new computer program. Don't base your decisions solely on reviews without trying the system or software yourself.

■ If possible, spend some time working with a system before you buy it. Take a roadtrip to computer stores in your area and try current systems and software before you buy anything. No matter what the literature says, if you're not comfortable with the keyboard, the mouse, or the computer itself, you're not going to be happy when you get it home.

■ Although you don't need to buy a state-of-the-art system, don't buy something that is antiquated, either. Make sure that the system you purchase will be supported; that is, that parts and service will be available for that computer as long as you need it.

Demon-strations

Create a Can-Do List

Think about the types of things you do now that take up too much time or seem like too much effort. Then create a wish list of computer tasks your ideal system would accomplish:

1. Write down ways you work with text.

2. Write down ways you work with numbers.

3. Write down any tasks you perform that involve drawing, drafting, or designing.

4. Write down any other tasks you can think of (project management, communications, data management, etc.).

Create a Can't-Do List

Consider the things your computer won't be able to do that might be important to you from the start. Use a scale from one to ten—with one being lowest and ten being highest—to rate how important each of the following issues is to you. (You can use this list later to interrogate unsuspecting salespeople.)

- Compatibility with other computers
- Ease of use
- Ability to "grow"
- Wide range of features
- Ability to use many popular programs

Summary

This introductory encounter has explored some of the positives and negatives you'll find in your computer experience. Although computers can really help you streamline many of the tasks you now perform by hand, the flip side is a confusing, changeable mess of computer options that you must sort through before deciding on a system. (If you're inheriting a system, you're both fortunate and unfortunate: fortunate because you don't have to wade through current computer literature and make a decision, but unfortunate because you have no choice.) The next encounter helps you pin down the ways in which you will use your computer.

Exorcises

1. The first personal computer was the _____.

2. True or false: You can add any number of items to any computer.

3. Describe the main complaint of early PC users.

4. What was the first computer designed to be easy to use, and how was it different from PCs?

5. True or false: It's always best to buy the latest technology available.

How Will You Use Your Computer?

Goal

To determine specifically how you will use the computer you purchase (or inherit).

What You Will Need

A few minutes and a general interest in the kinds of tasks you may be using your computer to perform.

Terms of Enfearment

applications	database
software	graphics
word processing	project managers
spreadsheet	CAD
modem	communications
E-mail	

Briefing

When the first personal computers appeared on the scene, they weren't capable of much—not by today's standards, anyway. Besides the fact that the computer hardware itself was not very powerful, personal computers were further limited by the fact that there just weren't many programs available. And, although the hardware is necessary, our computers are worthless without software.

A Look at What's Out There

Today, you'll find programs for every imaginable task you might perform on your computer. From running a grocery store to writing a symphony, programs exist to help us computerize the process. You'll find computer programs that allow you to use your computer for all these tasks (and more):

- Writing letters, reports, books, brochures, etc. You can also create form letters and have the program insert customer names and addresses at the appropriate points (known as *mail merging*). This type of application is known as *word processing*.

- Working with financial information (accounts receivable and payable, payroll, taxes, financial analyses, projections, balance sheets, etc.). You create these financial models by using a *spreadsheet* program.

- Keeping track of information, in the form of client names and addresses, project information, inventory, etc. Programs that allow you to enter, organize, and print information are known as *database* programs.

- Publishing materials such as brochures, fliers, business cards, stationery, quarterly reports, magazines, etc. Creating a professional-looking publication with a personal computer requires the use of *desktop publishing* software (see fig. 2.1).

- Designing and illustrating a variety of works. The personal computer has in recent years become one of the most important tools in a graphic artist's toolkit. To create graphics on your personal computer, you use *graphics* software, which may also be referred to as *paint* or *draw* programs (see fig. 2.2).

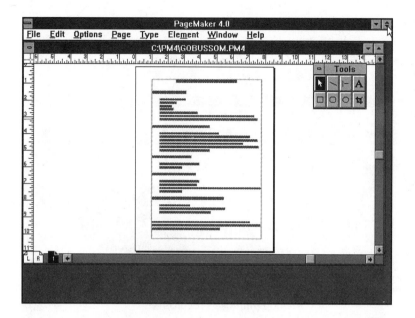

Figure 2.1
You can publish materials with desktop publishing software.

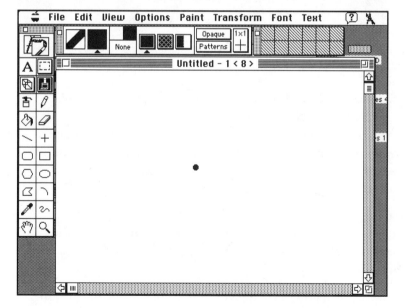

Figure 2.2
Paint and draw programs are easy to use (and fun, too).

■ Creating presentations that mix text and graphics. Gone are the days of the overhead projector and acetate sheets; now you can use your personal computer to create attention-grabbing presentations, complete with full color, cool text styles, and special visual effects (see fig. 2.3). This type of program is known as *presentation graphics* software.

Figure 2.3
Fear of presentations? Not with the right program.

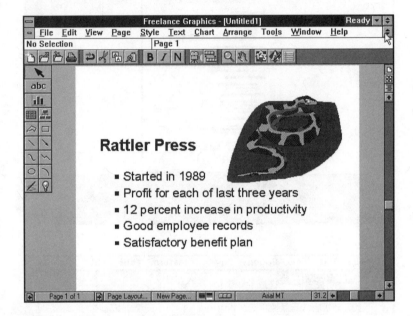

Managing projects and allocating resources. A number of popular programs are available to help you get and keep yourself organized. Known as *project managers* or *schedulers*, these programs allow you to divide projects into parts and to organize work flow and personnel on-screen. This type of program can include calendars, day-timers, and other types of planning software.

Drafting and architectural design. This type of software, known as *CAD* (or *computer-aided design*) applications, are highly specialized design programs that allow users to create plans, blueprints, and schematics, among other things.

Teaching. The personal computer gained its first major audience in school systems throughout the country with the almost overnight success of the Apple II. Since that time, personal computers—Apple and PC—have been used in schools and homes to educate young and old alike. *Educational* software is extremely popular and diverse, ranging in topics from Spanish lessons to the history of the world to learning about ecology. Young (and not so young) people enjoy games with favorite characters like Mickey Mouse, Bert and Ernie, and Big Bird. For almost every subject taught in schools today, you can find a software program to support it.

■ Game-playing. Games, too, are big business. You'll find any number of arcade-style games available for your PC, as well as puzzles, mysteries, card games, and a gazillion other choices. Although few people purchase a computer simply for the games they can play, the prospect does make computer work a bit more interesting.

■ Linking to other computers. If your computer has a device called a *modem* and a kind of program known as *communications* software, you have everything you need to hook up to another computer around the corner or across the country. Many people call up large, commercial mainframe computers (known as *information services*) to get a variety of information, including up-to-the-minute stock quotes, technological research findings, world news, health information, home and family forums, games and entertainment, vacation planning, and home shopping (really!). Communications software is also used to send and receive *E-mail* (electronic mail), which is a computerized version of a messaging service.

Many people use more than one of these different applications. You might, for example, use a word processing program to write letters, a spreadsheet program to keep track of payroll, and a database program to store client names and addresses and personnel data. You also might use a desktop publishing program to create the advertising fliers you send out monthly, a graphics program to create your company logo, and E-mail so that your clients can leave messages for you easily.

Far and away, however, the biggest reason people invest in a computer is that they have at least one application need from the big three: word processing, spreadsheets, or database. Most business users will have some involvement with one of these three applications, although others in the application group may take equal shares of time. The Big Three are discussed in the following sections.

For more information on the various software types, see the 15th Encounter.

Word Processing

Everybody writes. Some people agonize over their writing more than others. If you're one of those people who sweats out each word you put on paper, you're going to love word processing.

Word processing takes the sting out of writing—whether you're creating a memo, a letter, a report, or a book—because anything you write can be changed easily. Make a mistake? Delete it! A few keystrokes and that glaring error is gone—no correction fluid or tape necessary.

If you read through your work and find out that you've discussed things out of order, you don't have to throw it out and start again: you can move the paragraphs around to fix the problem — an electronic cut-and-paste job which is much less hassle than ripping a page from the Smith-Corona and trying again.

Formatting on the age-old typewriter can be a bear, as well. How many tabs was in that address? How many lines down was the salutation? Writing with your personal computer makes formatting simple, especially with some programs (like Microsoft Word) that help you build in a format so that all the indents and spacing can be controlled with a few simple keystrokes (see fig. 2.4).

Word processing can also enhance the quality of your work. Not sure about the spelling of a word? Let the spelling checker take care of it for you (see fig. 2.5). Most popular word processing programs include spelling checkers that often have 100,000-word dictionaries and give you the choice of creating your own customized dictionary. Additionally, some word processing programs have a thesaurus and a grammar-checker.

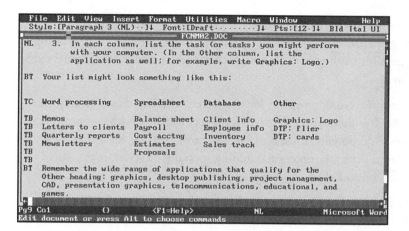

Figure 2.4
Formatting and making corrections is easy with word processing.

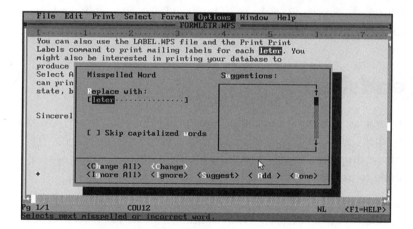

Figure 2.5
Most word processors can check your spelling for you.

But perhaps the handiest benefit word processing brings to your desktop is the wonderful world of reusable data. Have you ever had to retype a letter several times? What a waste of time—typing something you've already typed. With word processing, you can lose that bad habit forever. Because the information you type is saved in a file, you can use the data over and over again in other documents without retyping it. After the text is saved, it remains in the file, ready for you to use tomorrow or next year.

Many business users enjoy the mail-merge capabilities often offered in popular word processing programs. Mail merging is the process of creating form letters (or mailing labels) into which names and addresses are merged at print time.

Most word processing programs look on-screen the way they look in print; that is, the document you create will look very much like what you compose on-screen. Additionally, most of these programs give you the option of printing in different typefaces and adding special type styles, such as bold-face, italics, or underline.

All these features allow you to work faster and smarter, but the single biggest benefit is how simple documents are to change. If you make a mistake using your typewriter, you have to rip the page out and start again. If you make a mistake on-screen, you can go right to it, fix it, and print it—all in a matter of seconds.

Spreadsheets

And then there are the numbers people. Some people love numbers—day and night, they figure, analyze, recalculate. They love to say things like "Yes, but what if we dropped the price two cents for 16 months?" and then run off to their desks to use their $300 calculators.

There are also those of us who refuse to balance our checkbooks (using religious conviction as an excuse). Truth is, numbers scare us. We hated math in fifth grade, and we hate it more now.

Spreadsheets have features that will please both groups. First and foremost, spreadsheets cut off a large portion of the error margin. How many times have you pressed 9 on the calculator when you meant to press 8? That can really mess up your balance sheet. If you're working on-screen, you can see the numbers you're adding. If a 9 sneaks in, you can weed it out before you total.

The spreadsheet also includes features called *functions* that perform certain calculations for you. You enter these functions directly in the spreadsheet so that the program takes over the calculations for you. You don't have to worry about typing numbers or figuring percentages or any other nonsense. Again, like text in a word processing file, the data you enter in a spreadsheet stays in the file so that you can use it again and again (see fig. 2.6). No refiguring; no re-entering. Do it once and be done.

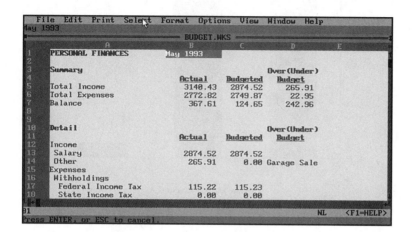

Figure 2.6
Spreadsheets make it easy to count your chickens before they hatch.

Spreadsheets also offer graphing features. Although a spreadsheet is made up of columns and rows of numbers (and text labels), a graph provides a quick-look way to see data trends. For example, if your business increased profit by 20 percent in the last quarter, that increase will be much more obvious in graph form than in numeric form (see fig. 2.7). All popular spreadsheet programs provide graphing capabilities.

If you're working with a spreadsheet, you can also create printouts—called reports—of your financial data. Need to print a balance sheet? Accounts payable or receivable? You can design your own format and print the reports the way you need them. Some spreadsheet programs also allow you to spruce up the reports you print by choosing professional-looking typefaces and incorporating graphs in the report itself. Totalling columns in a report is no problem; all spreadsheet programs provide a number of printing options that you can set to get the type of report you need.

Figure 2.7
*All popular spread-
sheet programs
have graphing
capabilities.*

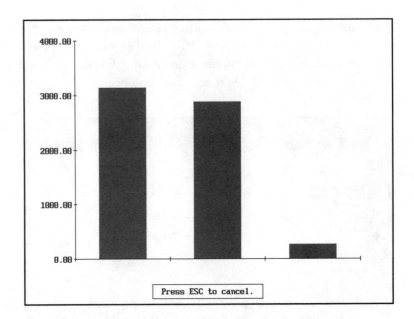

Press ESC to cancel.

Database

You already use a database, in one form or another. The Yellow Pages is one
example of a database; your Rolodex is another. Any collection of data is
technically a database. A database program allows you to enter information
and organize it in any way that makes sense to you. You might enter client
information—name, address, city, state, ZIP code, phone, etc.—in one
database and keep track of your company's inventory—part number,
quantity, cost, date ordered—in another database.

A database program enables you to create a data-entry form, setting up the
items you need. After you create the form, you can enter the data (see fig.
2.8). Most database programs allow you to create databases of any size—up
to the limit of your computer's disk storage.

After you enter the information, you need some method of organizing it the
way you want it. Database programs allow you to sort the data, arranging
clients, for example, alphabetically by last name, numerically by ZIP code,
etc.

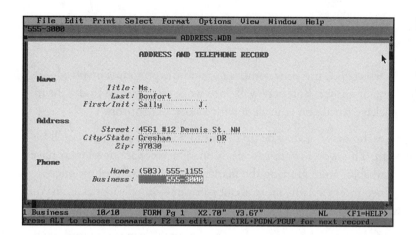

Figure 2.8

*You enter informa-
tion into the
database by using a
data-entry form.*

Another feature of database programs is the capability to search for specific
data items. Looking for all clients from Sacramento? You can search for
Sacramento among all the cities in your client database, producing a list of
clients in the selected area.

After you find the data items you want, you may want to print a report.
Database programs generally offer a variety of print options and report
formats. Similar to spreadsheet reports, database reports give you the option
of printing information in many different ways.

They're Out To Get Us

The way in which you use your computer—and the programs involved—may not be your choice. You may walk into work one day and find a shrink-wrapped package sitting on your desk with a note: "Learn this."

In other cases, however, it may be up to you to select the program you'll be working with. This won't be an easy decision. The software developers have done a remarkable job of glutting the market with thousands of products. The 15th Encounter explains more about software—how it works, how you use it, how to buy it.

As you get ready to purchase (or use) your computer, keep your mind open to tasks you can computerize. Your wish list of possible computer jobs will help you recognize helpful software when you see it.

Demon-stration

Thinking about how you'll use the computer will help you (1) begin to explore the different kinds of programs you'll use and (2) start to consider the system that is right for your particular computer needs.

1. Draw four columns on a sheet of paper.

2. Write these headings in the columns: Word processing, Spreadsheet, Database, Other.

3. In each column, list the task (or tasks) you might perform with your computer. (In the Other column, list the application as well; for example, you could write *Graphics: Logo*.)

Remember the wide range of applications that qualify for the Other heading: graphics, desktop publishing, project management, CAD, presentation graphics, telecommunications, educational, and games.

Summary

This encounter has explained some of the things you might do with your computer, once you get up and running. Although most business computer users have some involvement with at least one of the Big Three applications (word processing, spreadsheet, or database software), many people use programs from other application areas, as well. You may find yourself using several programs from several application groups, whether you are the person responsible for purchasing programs or whether the programs are purchased for you.

Exorcises

1. Which program type is used to work with numbers?

   a. Word processing   c. Database

   b. Spreadsheet   d. Project management

2. Name three benefits of using a word processing program.

3. A database program helps you _____ information.

4. True or false: Only three types of applications are used in business settings.

5. Name four program types (not including the Big Three).

Understanding the Ads

Goal

To help you understand the terminology used in computer advertisements.

What You Will Need

Access to a few computer ads and a healthy sense of skepticism.

Terms of Enfearment

RAM	local bus
cache	hard drive
expansion slots	accelerated video
notebook	handbook
laptops	desktop
trackball	backlit monitor
full-page monitor	

Briefing

If you are responsible for purchasing your own computer and have been spending time between the covers of popular computer magazines, you may feel swept up in a sea of computer jargon. You look through the ads and almost drown in the acronyms. What's a RAM? Are you supposed to know what MHz, 386SXL, IDE, CPU, and EISA stand for? How can you tell whether the system they are advertising is the one for you?

This encounter helps you translate the strange descriptions in the computer ads so that you'll know what you're looking for when your own time to purchase draws near. If your system was (or will be) purchased for you, this encounter will help you find out about the capabilities of your computer.

What Are They Saying?

Ads for PCs and Macintoshes differ slightly in the way the products are presented. PC ads tend to cover absolutely every feature possible in a bulleted list; Mac ads concentrate on the three or four most important items. Generally, however, most items overlap in both camps.

For example, consider the following items from a recent ad for a PC:

PC 486DX/33

★ **33 MHZ 80486**

★ **4M RAM**

★ **212M hard disk**

★ **6 expansion slots**

★ **dual floppy drives (3.5 and 5.25)**

★ **512K video RAM**

★ **Ultra VGA monitor**

Now take a look at information from an ad for a comparable Mac system:

Macintosh IIci

➥ *33 MHZ 68030*

➥ *5M RAM*

➥ *212M hard drive*

➥ *Seiko 14-inch monitor*

➥ *cache card*

➥ *Key Tronic MacPro Plus extended keyboard*

As you can see, most of these items at least sound similar. But what are they and how do you tell if that's what you want? The following section explains the different features listed in computer ads.

What Does It Mean?

33MHZ. This is a shorthand form for 33 MegaHertz and is used to rate the speed of the machine. 33 MHz is a pretty fast machine, considering that the early PCs operated at a little under 5 MHz. Both PC and Macintosh systems offer systems that clock in at this speed, with some lower (16 or 25 MHz) and some higher (50MHz). The overall speed of the computer, in large part, depends upon the microprocessor used.

80486 (**68030** in the Mac ad). This is the number of the microprocessor, the single most important chip in the machine (see fig. 3.1). The microprocessor, which is also called the CPU (central processing unit), is the brain of the computer. Early PC microprocessors were produced by Intel: the 8088, the 80286, and the 80386. Although the 80486 is the current standard, rest assured that the 80586 will be here soon. Each succeeding microprocessor is faster than the preceding one. The Macintosh family uses a different microprocessor, produced by Motorola, based on the 68000 series. The low-end Macs (Mac Classic and PowerBook 100) use the 68000; mid-range Macs (Classic II; PowerBooks 140 and 170; and Macs LCII, IIsi, and IIci) use the 68030; and high-end Macs (the Quadra 700 and 950) use the 68040.

Figure 3.1
The microprocessor is a single chip inside the computer.

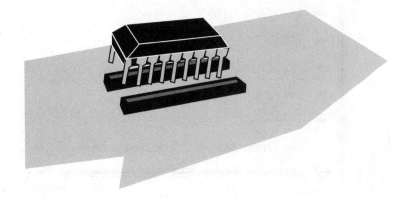

4M RAM. RAM is an acronym for *random-access memory,* which is the type of memory your computer uses to store the program(s) and data you work with during a session at your computer. Although the microprocessor and the RAM chips are all chips (also called *ICs,* for *integrated circuits.*), they are different kinds of chips (see fig. 3.2). The microprocessor does the actual "thinking" that goes on during a worksession, and the RAM chips store the programs and data in use.

Figure 3.2
The microprocessor chip and the RAM chips are different kinds of chips.

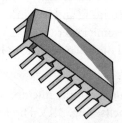

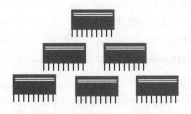

The CPU is a single chip responsible for all processing.

RAM chips are ICs that store programs and data.

When you start a program, the computer loads it from disk storage into RAM. The more RAM your system has, the better chance you have of running multiple programs and working with large files at a quick pace; less RAM can slow things down and make it impossible for you to have several programs or files open at one time. The original PCs had only 64K (roughly 64,000 bytes of information), but today's standard systems are sold with no less than 2M (that's approximately two million bytes of information). Most systems sold today have at least 4M of RAM, with enough room for you to add RAM to total 32M.

> For more information about computer speed and memory, see the 10th Encounter, "A Look Inside the Computer."

212M Hard Disk. This line of the ad actually gives you two different types of information: (1) that the computer has a hard disk, a device that stores your programs and data; and (2) that the hard disk can hold up to 212 million bytes of information.

> In general terms, a byte is roughly equivalent to one word of information. Technically, a byte is eight bits. But what's a bit? See the 10th Encounter for more information.

The first hard disks stored only 10M (that's ten million) bytes of information, but computer users—at the time—thought it would be impossible to use up *all that storage*. Today, 120M is the norm, with capacities on the huge side of that becoming more popular (see fig. 3.3). Why the big difference between then and now? Our programs are bigger, and we've got more of them. Our data files are more complex and take up more room. It's not unusual for a good program to take up more than 20M of hard disk space. And that doesn't even count your data files. The 11th Encounter explains more about disk drives and storage space.

Figure 3.3
The original hard disks stored only a fraction of the information that can be stored on today's standard hard disks.

Original hard disk (10M)

Today's standard (120M)

Some computer dealers offer data compression software that compresses the data on the hard disk. This can turn a 120M hard disk, theoretically, into a 240M hard disk. One such manufacturer is Austin Computer Systems, which offers the SuperStor data compression utility with its 386 Notebook computer.

6 Expansion Slots. This sounds a little too close to "techie" for comfort, but it's an important consideration when you're selecting the computer you'll spend a good portion of your life using. A computer needs to be able to grow with you. And the way your computer will grow in the future is by adding items to the now-vacant expansion slots. If the ad says six, the computer has spots for six additional items. (The items could be an additional memory card or cards for extra computer equipment like a printer, a mouse, a modem, etc.)

Dual Floppy Drives. Floppy drives provide you with another means of storing your programs and data. The disk drives—which come in two varieties, 5.25-inch and 3.5-inch—read and write data from the surface of disks that you insert in the drive opening (see fig. 3.4). Most PCs sold today offer dual disk drives, one of each size. Macs, on the other hand, use only 3.5-inch drives as their standard. The 11th Encounter explains how disk drives work.

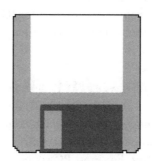

Figure 3.4
*A 5.25-inch and a
3.5-inch disk.*

512K Video RAM. In the years since the earliest personal computers, the race for the fastest and best has been running at an ever-increasing pace. One of the relatively new developments is the addition of video RAM. This is special memory included on the video adapter (the device inside your computer that sends the picture to the screen) that accelerates the screen display. Not all computers—or adapters, for that matter—offer video RAM. 512K is the amount (approximately 512 thousand bytes) of RAM included on the adapter.

Ultra VGA Monitor. This line in the ad vaguely describes the screen included with your system. Notice that in this particular description, the brand name of the monitor has been omitted. Early monitors had pretty shoddy displays, but we didn't know the difference because they had no competition. Today's monitors are sleek, sharp, sophisticated machines in themselves. You can find monitors in a variety of shapes and sizes.

Jargon alert: Portrait, landscape, full-page, two-page, and oversized are all terms used to describe different monitor types. VGA is the current standard, with better-than-the-norm displays offered by SuperVGA (often written SVGA), Extended VGA, and the top-of-the-display-line Ultra VGA. For more about monitors and display quality, see the 12th Encounter.

Cache Card. This option was listed in the Mac advertisement but not in our chosen PC ad. (Sometimes you'll see *64K cache* in a new PC ad.) A *cache* is a special portion of memory that runs off a few high-speed memory chips (different from the chips used for RAM). The cache can significantly speed up the processing of the computer.

What *Didn't* They Tell Us?

Several things in this particular computer ad missed someone's attention. Is there a mouse with the system? If you're considering the Macintosh, the answer is yes. For most PC systems, unless the ad gives the mouse a little bullet of its own, you have to purchase the mouse separately.

What about printers? Few computer systems are offered with printers. The exception is the case when you purchase a package deal (like a multimedia or desktop publishing workstation, for example), and the manufacturer builds in all the pieces you'll need to accomplish that particular goal (see fig. 3.5). Most times, however, you'll be on your own to choose a printer.

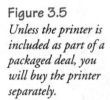

Figure 3.5
Unless the printer is included as part of a packaged deal, you will buy the printer separately.

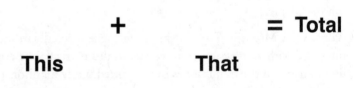

This   +   That   = Total

Modems? Some ads claim "built-in FAX/modem" as part of the offered price, and other manufacturers hold the carrot out as part of an optional deal. Other ads will offer traditional modems—with no FAX capability—as part of their computer systems. In most cases, however, the modem is sold separately.

A keyboard? Yes, virtually all computer systems come with a keyboard of one kind or another. Generally, in PC ads, you'll see 101-key Enhanced keyboard. Macintoshes are quite at home with the Apple Extended keyboard, which is similar in layout to its PC counterpart. (For more about keyboards, see the 8th Encounter.)

What About Other Computer Types?

Although this encounter has explored a typical computer ad for a desktop system, you'll find other types of systems as you ruffle through the computer pages. Laptops, notebooks, and even palmtop computers are popular for on-the-go computing.

Laptop computers are considered those ranging from 10 to 15 pounds, with a handle for "easy" carrying. Notebooks are the lite version, downscaling to between 6 and 9 pounds with significantly smaller dimensions and no handle necessary. Palmtops, like the Wizard, are hardly bigger than calculators, fitting easily into a briefcase (or, perhaps, large jacket pocket). Another new type of undersized computer, the HandBook (offered by Gateway 2000), weighs in at just under 3 pounds and measures out to be only 6-by-10 inches, smaller than a standard sheet of notebook paper.

The same basic terminology will apply to these computer types, although you may see an additional line or two for things like "built-in trackball" (a mouse-like device that helps you position the cursor on the screen) or "3.5-hour battery," meaning that you can use the computer for three-and-a-half hours before the thing dies.

Many laptops come with trackballs built into the system itself (just above the keyboard) or offer trackballs that clip on to the side of the keyboard for easy access (see fig. 3.6). When you use a mouse, you move the mouse around on the desktop to position the cursor, but with a trackball, you move the small ball in the center of the device (see fig. 3.7). Trackballs are used on laptops because there may be times when you're literally working in your lap—and then where would you put a mouse?

Figure 3.6
Some laptops include built-in trackballs instead of mice.

Figure 3.7
To move the cursor on the screen, you rotate the small ball in the center of the trackball.

One of the downsides of laptop computing is the relatively short period of time it's available. You charge up the battery and have three (or possibly four, if you're lucky) good hours of computer use. And that's it, until you've had a chance to recharge the battery pack. What happens when your flight circles O'Hare for four hours? The computer goes dead (unless you brought along a spare, fully charged battery pack). You may see a line in your computer ad for an AC adapter. If they offer it, buy it.

> If you're an international traveler, don't bank on being able to use your AC adapter while you're in your room overlooking the Seine. Be prepared to take charged-up battery packs—and plenty of them—when you're traveling to new places.

Important considerations like the microprocessor, available RAM, number of disk drives, hard disk storage, and any expansion slots will be covered in any ad for laptop or notebook computers (see fig. 3.8). As far as the monitor is concerned, you'll see the same standard—VGA—with a few additional adjectives (grayscale, backlit, super-twist, and anti-glare).

LAPTOP 386
22 MHz 386!
80M hard drive!
4M RAM!
Backlit monitor!
3 hr. battery
Fax/modem!
Built in Trackball!

Figure 3.8
An ad for a notebook computer.

Grayscale monitors are black-and-white monitors capable of displaying (usually) 64 shades of gray. These monitors are great for text work and provide a sharp contrast, even on smaller screens.

A backlit monitor is the monitor of choice for a laptop—as opposed to an LCD monitor—because it relies on a light from within for its display. By contrast, an LCD (liquid crystal display) monitor relies on room light for the display. LCDs can be hard on the eyes and a real pain in a room that's too dark or too light.

Super-twist refers to the way the monitor is connected to the laptop's system unit: A super-twist can take more wear and tear than a standard joint. Anti-glare means that the screen is coated with a special material that keeps the shine off the screen, even in direct sunlight.

They're Out to Get Us

Of course, whether you're buying a car, a house, or a computer, the ads make everything look good. Everyone is smiling; all the systems look sleek and sophisticated. You can't *help* but be smarter after you have one of these babies sitting on your desk, right? That's what the manufacturers would have us think.

But there are things we can't tell from an ad in a computer magazine. We can't tell, really, what the system looks like. We don't know how the keyboard feels. We won't know until later that the trackball is difficult to use, that the space bar sticks, and that the release button on the 3.5-inch drive is hard to push. We can't tell, from the ads, that the Reset button is in a place where we will hit it by accident. All these tidbits of knowledge come only from day-in, day-out computer experience.

If you're considering buying a computer sight unseen, here's a bit of advice: Call the company and ask everything you can think of. Then call them back and ask again. Make sure that you get answers—straight ones—to questions like these:

- What happens if you guys ship the computer out here and I don't like it?

- What if the computer doesn't work right?

- What if it breaks?

- What's your technical support policy? (Most reputable places will offer at least one year of technical support at no extra charge; some places offer up to three years.)

- What's the average length of time it takes to get a computer repaired? (You don't want your broken system sitting on their shelves for three months, awaiting surgery. Some companies will send out a loaner system while you wait for yours to be repaired. Ask.)

- Are there any additional costs? (The AC adapter may cost extra, and laptop or notebook cases may also be an extra charge. Ask also about shipping, which may be quite a fee if you're receiving a system with several pieces.)

Demon-strations

Evaluating a Computer Ad

The first step in evaluating a computer ad is, of course, finding one. You aren't limited only to computer magazines, either; many popular general interest and business magazines push personal computers.

1. Read through the ad carefully.

2. Check the microprocessor and determine what the speed is. (*Hint:* PCs use the 80x86 family of microprocessors, and Macintoshes use the 68030 family. The speed of the microprocessor is listed in MHz.)

3. Does the system have a hard disk? If so, how many megabytes (written as M or, sometimes, MB) of storage are available? Are any other sizes of hard disk offered? Does the manufacturer include a compression utility?

4. How much RAM does the system come with? Can you add additional RAM? Up to how much?

5. What kind of disk drive does the system have? Would this size be compatible with any other systems you might be trading files with?

6. What kind of monitor is included with the system? Is there additional video RAM on the graphics card? How large is the monitor?

7. Does the system come equipped with a mouse? A trackball? Will you need either item to work with your programs?

8. Does the system come with any software included in the deal? If yes, what kind? Would the program be useful for your business or personal computing?

9. Does the company offer technical support? For how long? At your place or theirs? Do they give loaners?

Grow-Your-Own Computer Ad

Now that you know how to read what the manufacturers are offering, you can get an idea of the types of things that are important to you by writing your own ideal ad.

1. What size system are you considering (desktop, laptop, notebook, or palmtop)? For the more adventurously creative: Draw the system you want at the top of the page.

2. Write your own ad copy, with the type of items and capabilities you want. Include all items that are important to you. For example, if you want a hard disk, write how much storage you want, like this:

   ■ 120M hard disk

3. Add a line about technical support (fair and reasonable technical support—no use adding "Free 24-hour tech support for as long as you own your machine" because, as they say, it just ain't gonna happen).

4. After you've finished your ad, stick a big price tag somewhere conspicuous. This amount should reflect what you'd be willing to pay if all the other items fell into place just the way you want them.

Some computer dealers offer to match any ad you bring in. Your home-grown version probably won't qualify. It will, however, help you target the type of system features that are most important to you and provide you (and any salesperson you might deal with in the future) with some kind of starting point.

Summary

This encounter helped you decipher some of the computerese you'll find running rampant through computer ads. What do most current systems offer and what difference does it make? Hopefully, you've found some of your answers here and are prepared to move on to the next encounter in which you determine what qualities in a computer are most important for the work that you'll be doing.

Exorcises

1. True or false: PC and Macintosh ads are completely different.

2. What two pieces of information does the following line provide?

   25 MHz 386

3. Write the appropriate letter in the blank:

   _____ MHz   a. Memory

   _____ 512K   b. Device that stores large amounts of programs and data

   _____ expansion slots   c. 212 million bytes

   _____ 4M RAM   d. Memory on the video card that speeds up screen display

   _____ Ultra VGA   e. MegaHertz, which measures the speed of the machine

   _____ 486   f. 512 thousand bytes

   _____ 212M   g. Room for your system to grow

   _____ video RAM   h. A segment of special high-speed memory that makes processing faster

   _____ hard disk   i. One kind of microprocessor

   _____ 64K cache   j. The current display standard

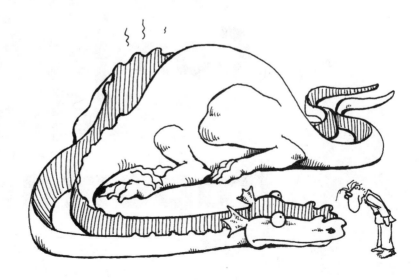

BILLY BOBS USED COMPUTERS

4th Encounter

Buying a Computer: What's Important?

Goal

To help you determine what computer features are important for your particular needs.

What You Will Need

A few minutes and the desire to make an educated decision about the type of computer you purchase or the way you use the computer you already have.

Terms of Enfearment

applications	mail-order
software	integrated packages
multimedia	

Briefing

What a horrible thing it would be to make a big decision on a whim and then regret it later. If you buy a computer because you like the way it looks, you may get it home and find out it is sadly lacking some important features you need for your daily computing. Better to do a little research—ask yourself a few questions—and analyze what you need in a computer before you go out and write that check. That way, you can make sure that the purchase is one that won't haunt you in the future.

Of course, if you're inheriting a system or getting one forced on you, the choice of models isn't up to you. You simply have to find out about the system you've got and make the best of it.

This encounter helps you determine what features are most important to you in the computer you buy. If you've already got the system and there's nothing you can do about it, this encounter will help you find out where, in the scope of computers, your particular system falls. Then, later, you can use the knowledge to perhaps add on to the computer you have or make some heavy-duty arguments for the purchase of one you really want.

The System: What Do You Want?

We might as well get the pie-in-the-sky wishes out of the way. Everyone wants a computer that takes care of everything: taxes, grocery shopping, babysitting, and letters to those relatives who call and make you feel guilty about not visiting. If you've got to use the blasted thing, it might as well make itself useful.

Get a group of computer addicts together and ask them to produce a "Want List," and you'll see things like 24-bit TrueVideo board, 600-dpi laser printer, SuperVGA two-page monitor, or 210M hard drive. (Don't even bother wondering what those items are.)

Your list is probably much different. You want a computer that is easy to use. You're looking for something that doesn't beep at you at every turn, that provides a little help along the way, that can accomplish all the vague things you hope it will do with as little trouble as possible.

The computer itself will have a lot to do with the way you use it. The Macintosh, for example, provides a hand-holding atmosphere that a generic PC may lack (see fig. 4.1). The friendliness of the machine, however, is not the result of the computer's hardware—the nuts, bolts, chips, and capacitors that make your computer work—but rather the effect of the operating system the machine uses.

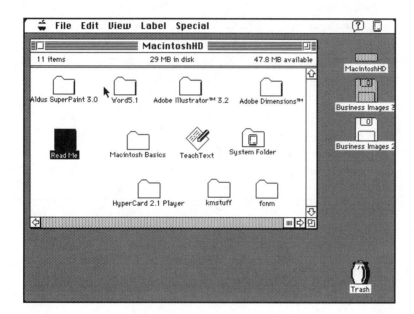

Figure 4.1
The Macintosh is known for its friendlier face.

Jargon alert. The *operating system* is a kind of program that translates what you want done into instructions the computer can understand.

The hardware of your computer brings up several different purchasing concerns. First and foremost, these issues are important:

- ■ Do you like the way the keyboard feels?

- ■ Is the monitor adequate for everyday use?

- ■ Does the computer run the software you need?

- ■ Does the system have enough memory to run the programs you need to run?

■ Is there enough disk storage space to hold all necessary programs and data?

■ Does the computer have room to add on other items (printer, mouse, modem, etc.)?

It's the old chicken-egg controversy: Should you get the software first and then choose the computer to run it, or do you choose a computer and then find the software you need? People line up on both sides. If you are getting a computer so that you can take work home from the office, you'll need to get a computer for home that can run the same programs and use the same files. That means that if you use a PC at work and want to take work home, get a PC. If the type of computer you select is solely your choice, investigate all major types of computers and the programs available for each. Then choose the system within your price range that supports the highest number of programs that interest you.

The Programs: What Do You Need?

The *tasks* you will accomplish with your computer actually depend on the type of programs you use. The programs that will run on your computer, however, depend on the type of computer you select. Macintosh computers, for example, run Macintosh programs. If the program you need to use in your work is available only for PCs, buying a Macintosh would be a mistake.

Some people use computers for specialized tasks. For example, even hard-core computer haters are usually somewhat enchanted by the new range of animation and multimedia possibilities that are now en vogue. Today, we've got multimedia programs that teach our kids about the rain forest, show us how to assemble automotive engines, and let us benefit from the work of research scientists all over the world. In this way, computers are providing us with a whole new—and more interesting—approach to educating ourselves and our children.

Jargon alert: Multimedia is a new area of computing that mixes video, sound, and special graphics to produce an on-screen presentation.

And games are good. Most people—even in times of great stress—will keep from beating their computers to death simply because they enjoy that occasional game of Solitaire or Tetris (see fig. 4.2).

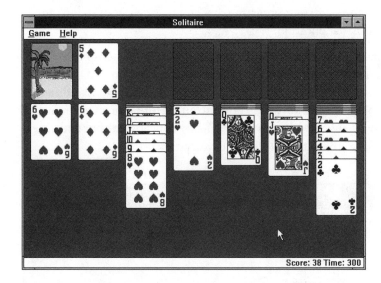

Figure 4.2
Everybody needs a little fun now and then.

But beyond cool special effects and games, computers are used for specific tasks by millions of people worldwide. What are they all doing? Writing letters, reports, and books; calculating extensive spreadsheets; entering client information; keeping track of inventories; designing presentations.

What will you do with your computer? The answer to this question will have some bearing on the type of system you eventually get. If you will use your computer only for writing letters to business contacts, the amount of memory your computer needs will be less than a user who will be producing elaborate desktop published materials. Likewise, you may need only a basic, relatively inexpensive monitor, while high-end graphics work would require a top-of-the-line monitor. If you're going to be entering information about thousands of clients, it's important that you make sure that you purchase a computer with enough disk storage space (a larger hard disk). If you will be using the phone lines to send reports in to the office, make sure that you get a modem.

You can see where we're going with this.

Knowing what type of programs you'll be using can help you identify some very important characteristics of your chosen system. The following list explains some of the different program types and tells you what to look for in a system for that application:

■ Word processing—You'll need a monitor that displays crisp characters (see fig. 4.3). Color or monochrome is a preference issue. Make sure that the screen doesn't waver, or you'll be buying stock in Excedrin before the year's out. (See the 12th Encounter for more about monitors.) You'll also need a printer (the quality depends on your audience) so that you can print the documents you create.

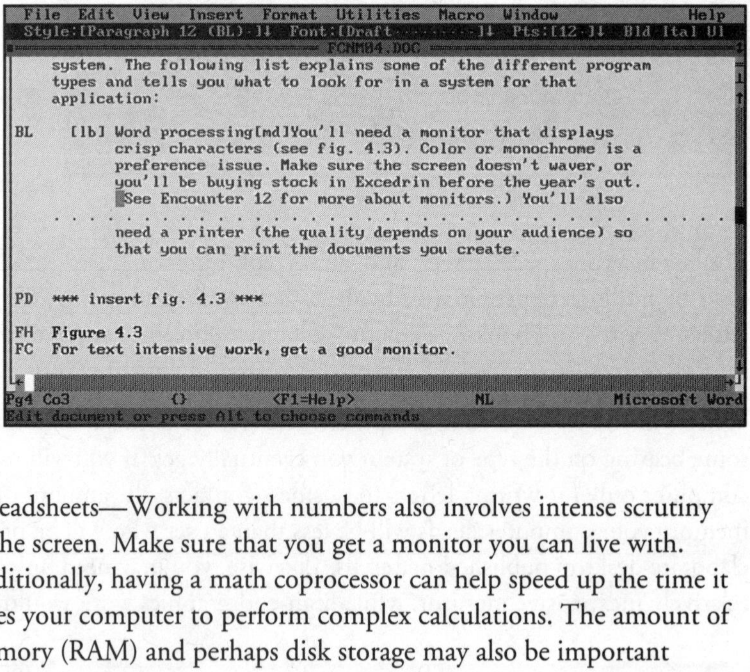

Figure 4.3
For text-intensive work, get a good monitor.

```
 File  Edit  View  Insert  Format  Utilities  Macro  Window            Help
 Style:[Paragraph 12 (BL) ]↓  Font:[Draft          ]↓  Pts:[12 ]↓  Bld Ital Ul
 ═══════════════════════════ FCNM84.DOC ═══════════════════════════
        system. The following list explains some of the different program
        types and tells you what to look for in a system for that
        application:

 BL     [lb] Word processing[md]You'll need a monitor that displays
             crisp characters (see fig. 4.3). Color or monochrome is a
             preference issue. Make sure the screen doesn't waver, or
             you'll be buying stock in Excedrin before the year's out.
             See Encounter 12 for more about monitors.) You'll also
        . . . . . . . . . . . . . . . . . . . . . . . . . . . . . . . . . . . . .
             need a printer (the quality depends on your audience) so
             that you can print the documents you create.


 PD     *** insert fig. 4.3 ***

 FH     Figure 4.3
 FC     For text intensive work, get a good monitor.

 Pg4 Co3        {}          <F1=Help>              NL        Microsoft Word
 Edit document or press Alt to choose commands
```

■ Spreadsheets—Working with numbers also involves intense scrutiny of the screen. Make sure that you get a monitor you can live with. Additionally, having a math coprocessor can help speed up the time it takes your computer to perform complex calculations. The amount of memory (RAM) and perhaps disk storage may also be important considerations, depending on the program you'll be using. (The 10th and 11th Encounters explain memory and disk storage in more detail.)

■ Data management—Keeping track of data, especially large volumes of data, makes having plenty of room to store it extremely important. Most programs you use to work with data—called *database programs*— also need a good amount of memory in order to process data and create reports.

■ Desktop publishing—A logical offshoot of word processing, desktop publishing lets you lay out and print any variety of published materials: newsletters, fliers, brochures, reports, books, and so on (see fig. 4.4). Desktop publishing means medium-to-high-end everything, including memory, disk storage, display quality, and print quality (you need your finished product to look professional, don't you?).

Figure 4.4
Desktop publishing requires a good system with an extra punch.

■ Graphics—The Macintosh has more true-blue advocates among artists than it has perhaps among any other applications group. The Mac, it seems, has a natural bent toward graphics work. Many extremely popular paint, draw, illustration, and animation packages are available for the Mac. PC users can find their share of artsy programs, but the number of PC artists pales in comparison to Mac graphics shops. If you're going to be doing graphics work, carefully consider which system you need in order to be compatible with clients and coworkers. Graphics uses a lot of memory and disk storage. And, as you might expect, having a terrific-quality monitor is a must (and a good printer doesn't hurt).

> With any computer you get, make sure that you have the option of adding more memory. Never buy a system you cannot expand.

You'll find many other types of programs out there: project managers, telecommunications programs, various disk and file utilities, integrated packages (that mix and match several of the application types in the preceding list)—the list goes on and on. Chances are, if you've been given a mandate to get a computer (or have decided yourself that it's time to buy one), you'll be using one of the applications included in the preceding list.

Preparing for the Event

Starting to get a grasp on what you need in a system? The next step is to organize your knowledge and begin educating yourself about the choices out there. Okay, you're going to be writing letters and working with a client list, so you know that you need a system with a good monitor, enough memory to run the programs you need, and a solid amount of disk storage space.

What's next? Research.

Watch the computer magazines for reviews (but don't believe everything you read). Talk to other people who have recently purchased a computer. What do they like about their new systems? What do they wish they'd known before they wrote the check?

Write down a list of questions you have about the system you're investigating. Then go out to the local computer store and try your hand at a few machines. Don't just tap around on the keyboard with a single finger; sit down and really type something—anything—to get the feel of the keyboard. Work with an application or two and see how the system feels. Is the monitor clear enough? How do the keys feel as you type? If there is anything about the system that bothers you, it's better to find out now, so give that computer a workout.

Make sure that you ask the Trusty Salesperson every question you can come up with. And if the salesperson knows less than you do about the system, do the old 360-degree turn and find another computer store—One with more knowledgeable salespeople.

Many people buy their computers from mail-order houses because the price is often much lower than their retail-store counterparts can offer. If you shop mail-order, you have a few other things to worry about: If the computer breaks down in six months, will the business still be there to fix it? Does the organization have technical support? What is the warranty on the machine you buy? Make sure that you get the answers to questions like these before you commit. Having a computer crash just a few months after purchase ranks right up on the stress scale with death and divorce—especially if the company that sold it to you has dried up and blown away in the meantime.

They're Out To Get Us

It's just another sign of our day and age: If you want to learn about different computer types, you have to educate yourself. Many computer retailers specialize in one or two lines of computers. When you go in to investigate your choices, the salesperson tells you that you're in luck—they have the perfect system for you. It just happens to be one of the two lines they stock.

Ask about a different type of computer and what happens? "Oh, no—you don't want that one. We've heard some bad things about that company." And they'll have a dozen more reasons why.

So how do you find the best system for your needs without being swayed by the commission-based bias of computer salespeople?

- ■ *Do your homework.* Read any available information on the types of computers you're investigating.

- ■ *Ask questions.* Talk to other computer users of various computers to find out their preferences (and remember to ask where they bought their systems).

■ *Have a good idea of the qualities you're looking for before you go in to the computer store.* Having a list of questions you want to ask and qualities that are important to you is also a good idea. This way you'll be less inclined to take the salesperson's word that the system she is pushing is the best one for your needs.

Demon-strations

Identifying Your Needs

Hopefully, you're starting to get an idea which features are more important to you than others. Here are some suggestions for fine-tuning that information:

1. Fold a piece of 8 1/2-by-11 paper in half lengthwise.

2. On one side of the sheet, write *Software* at the top.

3. On the other side, write the heading *Hardware.*

4. On the Software side, list the different programs you'll be working with.

5. On the Hardware side, list all the features important to the type of applications you will be using (for example, you might write Memory, Disk storage, Good monitor, etc.).

6. For each program, identify what you need in terms of hardware. For example, your list might look like this:

Software	*Hardware*
PageMaker	Memory: 2M
	Disk storage: 40M
	Monitor: VGA
Microsoft Word	Memory: 1M
	Disk storage: 40M
	Monitor: EGA

When you're finished, the list will tell you what kind of system features you need in order to run the software you'll be working with.

Going to the Horse's Mouth

The experience other people have with their computer purchases certainly won't be any guarantee as to how yours turns out, but going straight to the horse's mouth for trial-and-error advice can prove useful.

1. Ask coworkers about their personal preferences in computer families and style.

2. Talk to owners of different kinds of equipment to see what they think are the strengths and weaknesses of different brands.

3. Investigate purchasing experiences—mail-order, retail, etc.—to see whether other computer buyers would recommend one company over another.

Summary

Determining what you need before you buy is an important part of your overall computer experience. Start off on the right foot by analyzing what you need and doing some research before you buy. Get a system that can grow with you in the future and has the qualities you need now to run the programs you need.

Exorcises

1. Why is a good monitor necessary for word processing work?

2. The _____ is often selected for graphics work.

3. Explain why data storage is an important consideration for database applications.

4. True or false: Memory, disk storage, and display quality are three important features for desktop publishing applications.

5. Name three ways you can prepare yourself before you start computer shopping.

Dealing with an Inherited Computer

Goal

To help you determine what features—both hard-ware and software—are "possessed" by your system.

What You Will Need

The system you've inherited and any manuals or instruction sheets that go with it.

Terms of Enfearment

mouse pad	MS-DOS
printer cable	directories
operating system	diagnostics program
System 7.0	high-density
PC DOS	low-density

Briefing

This isn't the best possible circumstance for learning to use a computer: You walk into work on Monday morning to find atop your usually clean desk a rather large, unfriendly-looking computer. Beside the computer are a few disks with some name or another scribbled illegibly on the label.

Where did this thing come from and why is it here?

Some investigative work reveals that your boss has decided that you've been working in the Dark Ages and it's time to bring your tried-and-true method of manually balancing the books into the computer age. Sigh. Beaten, you sit down at your desk, looking at the blank face of this adversary. You pick up a disk and then put it down. You have no idea where to start.

Hardware: What Do You Have?

The first step is to find out what type of system you've got and determine what it can do. Hardware first.

Look for a name brand of some kind. Is there a little label proudly proclaiming IBM? What about a colorful little apple, indicative of the Macintosh line? Perhaps it's a more generic name like Magitronic, Everex, or Leading Edge. (If the name's been filed off, you may be in trouble.)

Often the computer tag, beneath the name, will show a number like 386SX-25. This tag will tell you two things: the type of microprocessor (80386) and the speed of the microprocessor (25 MHz). OK. Now you know whether you're dealing with a PC or a Mac.

Next, look for an obvious essential: the keyboard. Is there one? Is it hooked up for you, or is it sitting there all wound up in its own cord? (If it is not hooked up to the computer, see the 6th Encounter for instructions on putting your system together.)

What about a mouse? Not all systems need mice in order to run, although you won't get anywhere on a Macintosh without one. The mouse is still optional for PCs—even though some programs, like Microsoft Windows—are really designed to be used with a mouse. Look the mouse over. How many buttons does it have? Is it plugged in to the back of your computer? Does it have a mouse pad, so it won't skid across the desk?

> *Jargon alert:* A mouse pad is a spongy rectangular pad that is placed under the mouse. This helps the mouse move better across the desktop and gives you more accurate control for cursor placement on the screen. For more about mouse handling, see the 9th Encounter.

Do you see a printer anywhere around? Small or large, a printer is an optional necessity for producing letters, reports, and financial statements. If you have a printer, you should also have a *printer cable*—the long cord-like appendage that connects the printer and your computer system (see fig. 5.1). Is it connected?

Other printer considerations—things you can really wait to worry about until the 13th Encounter—include the paper, the printer ribbon (or toner), and extras like a sheet feeder. Make sure that someone takes you to the paper closet, helps you find the right size (your printer may take regular or wide-carriage paper), and shows you how to feed the paper through the machine before you try to print. Is the printer ribbon in there? Is it old, needing to be replaced, or new? If the printer is a laser printer, ask someone whether the toner has been recently replaced. Of course, you'll know whether the ribbon or toner is in good shape as soon as you start printing.

Figure 5.1
Printer essentials.

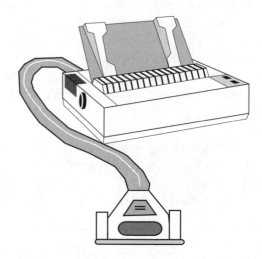

Other things that could get lost in the transfer from office to office include important items like power cords. Depending on your system, you may have one, two, or three power cords. Some computers use only one cord; it runs from the back of the computer to the wall outlet (or surge protector strip). Other computers have one cord from the computer and one from the monitor. Additionally, printers have their own power cords. Most power cords unplug from both ends (meaning they could be completely detached from your system). Make sure that you've got all the cords you need before you try to power anything up.

Software: What Does It Do?

After you've looked over the hardware, you're probably wondering what miracles of technology await you after you turn the thing on.

First, look around. Did any disks accompany your system? Are there any manuals that might give you a clue as to the programs endowed on this machine? For best results, find the previous owner and ask as many questions as you can. Request a demonstration, so the more experienced person can show you how to find the programs on the computer and give you the secret for exiting the programs after you start them.

You already know that the system includes at least one piece of software: the operating system. If your computer is a Macintosh, you will have several utility programs that accompany the basic operating system, System 7.0. The Apple menu, located in the top left corner of the screen, houses the options you may want to investigate (see fig. 5.2).

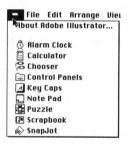

Figure 5.2
The Apple menu on the Macintosh screen.

In an earlier encounter, we mentioned that the operating system is the program that interacts between you and your computer, turning your commands and actions into instructions the computer can understand. Every computer must have an operating system in order to work. The current operating system standard for the Macintosh is System 7.0; for the PC, it's DOS. For more about operating systems, see the 17th Encounter.

If you are using a PC, your operating system is PC DOS or MS-DOS. (The primary difference between these two operating systems is that PC DOS is offered by IBM and MS-DOS is offered by Microsoft Corporation.) Depending on the version of the operating system on your machine, you also may have several additional programs built right into the software. DOS 6.0, the latest version, includes several small programs not available in earlier versions of DOS.

So how will you know what programs are included on your computer? If you are using the Macintosh, you'll be able to see little program icons in open folders on the screen. (You may have to double-click on the disk icon to display a folder. But we're getting way ahead of ourselves here; you don't learn to work with the mouse until the 9th Encounter. Just file this information for future reference.) If you're using a PC, you'll be able to see how the disk storage is divided up (and in doing so see where programs are stored) by using the DOS command DIR.

Determining what programs are on your computer requires that you turn on the system and begin to find your way around, which takes more talent than we've tapped so far. The best advice, before you've learned how to get things started yourself, is to ask someone familiar with the machine to do it for you. Then you can sit and observe from a safe distance before you're the one in the driver's seat.

Inheritance Tips

Really and truly, that system didn't just fall from the sky and appear on your desk. Someone had it before you did. Perhaps it was a person in another department, or maybe it was the purchasing agent, if the system is new. But if the computer comes to you already out of the box, rest assured that some human had his or her hands on it before it landed in your office.

Inheriting a computer is a different experience than purchasing one yourself. Your choices are limited—perhaps taken away altogether. The machine may be used, which means that it may have some "quirks" that are a result of the previous owner's habits. Even if the machine is new, if someone else set up the computer for you by installing the programs and setting up areas to store your data files (called *directories*), your experience will still be different than it would if you were doing it all yourself. Here are a few tips that relate specifically to the issue of inheriting a system:

- **Question the benefactor.** Who left you this present, and why? Why did they give it up? What did they do to it when they had it? Ask about the programs on the machine, and find out what the previous owner used the programs to do. See whether the benefactor ever had any trouble with the computer—a sticking A key? an on-line poltergeist?—and find out whether the thing might give you the same problem, too. Ask about any peculiarities about the system ("You have to start Word three times before it will take" or "Sometimes Windows crashes when you try to run Harvard Graphics") and get suggestions for avoiding those spots.

- **Get it in writing.** Make notes of your interview with the previous owner. Ask whether there are any instructions for the equipment and write down any suggestions you get. Make a list of all the pieces you're inheriting (so later, when you're asked to give the system to someone else, you'll know what you initially received). Find out whether the computer is under warranty anywhere or whether the system has recently been serviced. Get the phone numbers of people you can use as resources if the computer malfunctions or otherwise trips up.

> Anytime a computer changes hands—especially after a long trip—it's a good idea to have a technical support person check the system out. This check-up could involve the running of a simple program that looks for problems (called a *diagnostics* program) or it may involve cleaning and servicing of the entire unit.

- **Preserve the originals.** If your equipment was left for you along with software disks and manuals, make sure that you preserve the original disks and keep them in a safe place. Always work from copies of the original disks—called *backups*—so that if something destroys the copy, you've still got the originals left. The 17th Encounter explains how to make backup copies of your original disks.

They're Out To Get Us

Let's take the worst case scenario: You come in and find this computer. There's no one around who looks even remotely responsible. When you ask your employer about it, you find out that she purchased a few bargain-basement systems from another company that was closing up shop. No manuals, no backups, no warranty.

No one to ask.

What do you do? You're pretty much on your own, and "your own" isn't such a comfortable place. You don't know anything about this system except for its obvious physical characteristics, and neither does anyone else.

First, if possible, contact someone who knows something about computers. If neither you nor your coworkers have an acquaintance that can find his or her way around a computer, get out the Yellow Pages and call the nearest computer store. Ask about their technical support rates and find out about training. Most computer stores have at least one support technician who charges a (sometimes exorbitant) hourly rate to troubleshoot computer problems. Many stores today also have trainers who are available, on an hourly or seminar basis, to teach new computer users how to work with available software and hardware.

It's always possible that your boss doesn't want to shell out any more money for computer check-ups or training, especially when she thinks you can figure it out yourself. If that's the case, thank her for her vote of confidence, take a deep breath, and go on to the 6th Encounter.

Demon-stration

Previous Owner Interview

Hopefully, you'll inherit a system with a history—one that's easy to trace to the previous owner (who used her computer only after church on Sundays). After you've tracked her down—or, if you can't reach her, you've cornered a technical support person—try asking these questions (and remember to write down the answers for future reference):

1. Is there any warranty remaining on the system (and can it be transferred)?

2. When was the last time you had the system serviced?

3. How large is the hard disk?

4. How much memory is in the system?

5. What kind of monitor is this?

6. Are the disk drives high-density or low-density?

> *Jargon alert: High-density* and *low-density* are terms used to describe how much data can be stored on 3.5-inch and 5.25-inch disks. All you need to know about the disk drives, for now, is which type they are. For more about disk drives, see the 11th Encounter.

7. What programs, if any, are on the hard drive?

8. Have you ever had any trouble with the system?

9. Is there a mouse to go with the computer?

10. Are there any available expansion slots?

11. Is there a modem inside the computer?

It's very possible that, even though your inherited computer already includes several programs, you may wind up adding completely different programs and never using the ones already there. Nevertheless, it's helpful to know whether any of the existing software was giving the old user trouble, because someday the trouble may appear in your program when you least expect it!

Summary

An inherited computer brings with it a set of circumstances the computer purchaser does not experience. First, the choice of computer is beyond your control: there it is, and you have to make the best of it. Second, you must play sleuth to figure out who owned the system and what, exactly, you're dealing with. Remember to ask lots of questions about both the hardware and software (and write down the answers for future reference). And, if possible, find out whether the system has any "quirks" and is in need of servicing before you begin using it.

Exorcises

1. What's the first step in evaluating your inherited computer?

2. What is the name of the software that every computer must have?

3. What does the operating system do? (Choose the correct answer.)

   a. Allows you to type letters

   b. Performs necessary calculations

    c. Turns your commands into instructions the computer understands

    d. Manages the memory of your computer so it runs more efficiently

4. Name three tips for inheriting a computer.

5. True or false: You should have your computer checked out only when something is wrong.

6th Encounter

Getting Everything Set Up

Goal

To help you find just the right spot for your system and to set it up properly.

What You Will Need

Your system, along with any cables and power cords that came with it. (A desk would be nice.)

Terms of Enfearment

components	tower system
system unit	system stand
registration cards	paper feed
surge protector	connectors
ports	pins

Briefing

Now we're going to throw caution to the wind and assume that you've made your purchase (or made your peace with the computer purchased for you) and you're ready to assemble the darn thing. Perhaps someone has already connected all the pieces—called *components* in computer lingo—or the computer may still be in boxes.

Either way, you'll find tips in this encounter that will help you set up the system, place it where you want it, connect all the parts, and take an objective look at it when you're done.

> For the most part, we're talking desktop systems in this encounter. After all, you don't need to assemble a notebook computer—you just take it out of the box and use it. You don't need to choose a work area and worry about lighting, traffic, etc., because you'll be taking it with you and using it in airplanes, bus terminals, and at stoplights!

Figuring Out What You've Got

You've spent the last few encounters deciding on the type of computer that is most important for the work you do. Hopefully, all has gone well—the check cleared—and you're ready to unpack your new system.

PCs generally come to you in boxes—several boxes, in fact. The monitor is in one; the primary part of the computer, called the *system unit,* is in another; the keyboard is in another; and the mouse is perhaps enclosed in a see-through plastic package. You'll have other stacks of stuff: software, extra disks, computer manuals, and perhaps computer paper for the printer.

The number of pieces you have for your Mac depends on the Mac you bought. If you chose a Mac Classic, the monitor and system unit are packaged in one piece. Other Macs, like the Quadras, the II, or the LCs, are divided up in a fashion similar to PCs.

Your first step, before you even take anything out of the box, is to make a list of everything you've purchased. If you bought everything from the same company, you may have an invoice that will serve that purpose; but if not, make sure that you write everything down. After the initial shock of the expense wears off, you may find it difficult to remember the small things among those you purchased. Be sure to include important things like serial number, warranty, and manufacturer information. Your list should look something like this:

Date Purchased	Item	Serial Number	Manufacturer Name and Phone
7/1/93	386SX-25	RV33-4-5777	MGC (800-555-5555)
7/1/93	VGA monitor	45-3322TBS	Seiko (800-444-4444)
7/1/93	IST VGA board	2391VGA	RayKo (800-333-3333)
7/1/93	Bus mouse	1495T	Microsoft (800-222-2222)

Is anything missing? If so, contact your dealer (or mail-order company) immediately. Don't assume that a certain piece was back-ordered and will arrive eventually—take the initiative and find that missing piece.

Deciding Where It Should Go

One of the biggest tricks to setting up a good work area is choosing the right area. By the window or in the corner? Behind cubicle walls, where the temptation to daydream is minimized, or right out in the open, where everyone passing by will stop to chat?

In a traditional office environment, of course, your selection of work area may be much more limited. You may have four walls to choose from (or three and a door). How will you place the system? What side of the desk? Facing what and turned away from what? Do you need easy access to the phone? Even within a limited space, you still need to plan out the best place for your computer. After you choose the general arrangement, you must place the components so that they are easy and comfortable for you to use.

> If you're one of those people who has the option of facing a window (or facing away from it), you may find that having the window at your front is much better than having it at your back. Yes, the temptation is there (especially in early spring) to stare vacantly out the window and get nothing done. However, fighting that temptation will probably be less strenuous than squinting all day from the glare of natural light off your monitor.

First, narrow down your field of choices. If you're setting up a home office, choose the room for the computer. Make sure that the room has plenty of office resources—a phone line that can be reached easily, direct or indirect lighting (whichever you prefer), and plenty of electrical outlets. (Room for a desk would be nice, too.)

If you work in a cubicle or office, consider how you want the desk positioned: facing hallway traffic or facing away from it? Will your computer be linked with a cable to other computers? Or perhaps to a printer shared by several employees? The answers to these questions will have some bearing on where you place the desk, and, ultimately, the computer. Short computer cables may control the design of your office more than anything else.

After you've got the desk placed, you need to decide how you want the system arranged. Are you left-handed or right-handed? Your answer will determine where you should place the system unit and the mouse (if you will use one). Figure 6.1 shows a possible computer arrangement for a right-handed user; figure 6.2 shows the same equipment arranged as it might be for a left-handed user.

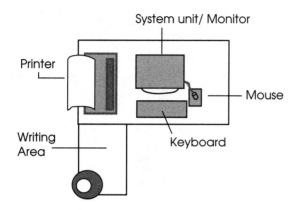

Figure 6.1
A right-handed computer arrangement.

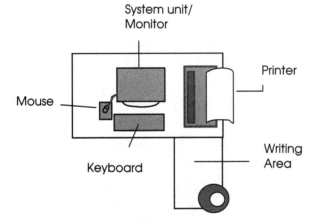

Figure 6.2
A left-handed computer arrangement.

As you unbox your system, remember to save anything that resembles a warranty card. Save them, fill them out, and send them in. This lets the manufacturer know that you've purchased their equipment and comes in handy in case you need technical support or service later.

Starting with the System Unit

Choosing that first spot—for the main part of your computer that houses the disk drives, called the system unit—is perhaps the biggest step (see fig. 6.3).

Figure 6.3

Setting the system unit.

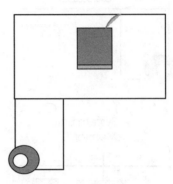

- Place the system unit so that the power switch is on the side you can reach most easily.

- Make sure that the computer's Reset button or on/off switch is not in a place where you can bump it accidentally.

- Especially if you work at home, take care to place the system unit so that tempting red Reset button is out of reach of little fingers.

- Arrange the unit so that you can insert and remove disks easily.

- If the unit is a *tower system unit* (meaning it stands on one end, vertically, instead of horizontally), you may want to place it under your desk.

If you are using a tower system unit, make sure that you also get a *tower stand* (a stand specially designed to anchor the system unit as it stands on end). The fall from the desktop to the floor may not be a big one for paperclips or pens, but it's a death drop for a system unit.

■ Make sure that there is an electrical outlet nearby so that you can plug in all the power cords from your system.

Many systems have more power cords than a single electrical outlet can handle. A device called a surge protector can take care of this. A *surge protector* is a specially designed strip of outlets that absorbs any surges or spikes in electrical power, thus protecting your plugged-in computer. Most surge protectors have between seven and ten outlets, allowing you to plug in your computer components as well as several other office necessities like lights, answering machines, and copiers.

Dancing on the Desktop

Your overall desktop will have much to do with the design of your layout (see fig. 6.4).

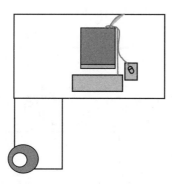

Figure 6.4
Plan for the rest of the desktop, too.

■ Leave room on your desktop for papers and books. Even though your computer will automate many of the tasks you do by hand, there still will be times when you need to look things up and work with papers. Make sure that you leave a comfortable amount of room for manual work.

- Put the mouse on the side of the computer you access most easily. If you are right-handed, put the mouse on the right. Left-handed? Put the mouse on the left. Make sure that the mouse cord is not squeezed tight; it should move freely along with the mouse. You should have enough room on the desktop to move the mouse comfortably.

- Maximum desk room is a choice commodity. Place the system so that it takes up the smallest amount of room necessary.

- Make sure that you can still reach the phone easily and move the phone away from the computer system and any loose disks you have lying about. (A telephone has a magnetic field that can erase or damage disks.)

- Be on the watch for any other items that are magnetized. For example, a magnetic paperclip holder is an innocent-looking offender.

Moaning Over the Monitor

You'll be staring into the square face of your monitor for a good percentage of your work day (see fig. 6.5). Plan for these items:

Figure 6.5
Adding the monitor.

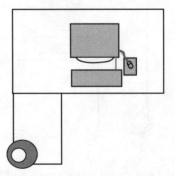

- Make sure that the light source is good enough for manual work but not so bright as to make working with the monitor difficult.

- The table or desk you use should be high enough so that the monitor is close to eye level.

If your desk or table is too short or too tall, there's not a lot you can do about it. You can, however, buy items that will bring your monitor more in line with your eye. Monitor stands can raise up screens that are too low; swivel and angle stands can let you tilt the monitor so that it is easy to see. Additionally, you can get anti-glare screens to fit over monitor faces that are not treated with an anti-glare surface.

■ Make sure that the monitor is placed so that it is well ventilated. Most monitors have vents on the sides, back, or top so that heated air can escape. If you place the monitor on a shelf that blocks the air flow or against a wall so that the ventilation is blocked, your monitor may fry. (Not a pretty sight—or smell.)

■ Consider other hazards in your area. The day after receiving her new PC, one officemate watered her hanging ivy. The plant appreciated the attention; her monitor didn't. The overfull plant spit water out the sides of the pot—into the monitor below. The result? A rather scary electrical ZAP! and several hundred dollars worth of repair costs.

Getting Peeved at the Printer

And now for the last big piece: the printer (see fig. 6.6). You may have more flexibility in placing the printer; it doesn't have to be right next to the rest of the system (although you may be limited by the length of the printer cable).

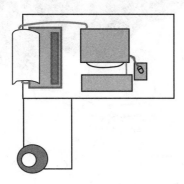

Figure 6.6
Adding the printer.

■ Make sure that the printer is close enough to connect to the system.

■ Place the printer so that the paper can move freely through the printer without being restricted.

■ Will the noise from the printer drive you crazy? Move it as far away as possible.

■ Think about where the paper will go after it passes through the printer. Will it pile up on the floor or fall back into the paper bin, obstructing the paper flow?

Take a few minutes to think about the system before you set it up. Extra planning now can save you some rearrange time later.

They're Out To Get Us

Few of us are interior designers. We're lucky to come up with some way to cram the desk, chair, phone, computer, printer, and a box of paper clips all into one little space. Make it look good? Forget it. Make it functional enough to not drive us crazy? Just barely.

There are people who design offices for a living, you know. They enjoy things like Rubik's Qubes and, probably, the 1040 Long Form.

For the Severely Cramped, computer manufacturers make smaller desktop systems. You'll see them in the ads as "small footprint" machines. Even if you down-size your system, you might not want to reduce the keyboard; a smaller keyboard may save you space, but it also may reduce your tolerance level. A few thousand extra typos because the keys are too close together is enough to cause even the sanest person to pitch the keyboard out a tenth-story window.

Whose Bright Idea Was This, Anyway? (Seven Office Don'ts)

So when you're thoroughly disgusted with your office and beginning to resign yourself to that unwelcome computer monopolizing the small amount of space you had to begin with, check the following Don'ts. If you don't see yourself here, relax. You've done the best you can with the space—and the system—you were dealt.

- Don't string cables in front of your computer (with the exception of the keyboard and mouse cables, which should run along one side of the system unit).

- Don't position a desk lamp so that it shines on the monitor.

- Don't put a regular system unit on its side like a tower unit.

- Don't push the system unit all the way back against the wall (the air flow will be obstructed).

- Don't place the system unit toward the front of the desktop so much that the keyboard is always sliding off the desk into your lap.

- Don't stack things on your monitor.

- Don't keep your refreshment center (Coke, coffee, M&Ms, and Danish) beside your computer.

Crimped Cables and Kooky Keyboards

You may find, after you power-up the computer (wondering when?), that some of your components act a little squirrelly. The printer doesn't print. The screen beeps at you, over and over. You type on the keyboard, and nothing happens.

The first thing you should do is take a good, long look at all the cables connecting your computer and its parts. All the computer components are connected through the use of cables—padded sets of wires that carry information from item to item. When you type at the keyboard, the keyboard cable carries the information to the system unit. When you print a document, the system unit sends information through the printer cable to the printer.

At the end of the cable is a connector (see fig. 6.7). The connector has little metal pins that plug into a receptacle on the back of the system unit.

Figure 6.7
A cable connector.

First, find the connectors for all the components (keyboard, mouse, monitor, and printer) and make sure that they are plugged in securely. Most connectors have small thumbscrews that you can tighten into place, ensuring that the connector won't pull loose over time. Yes, it's a pain and takes an extra 30 seconds but go ahead and tighten them down. Saves troubleshooting time later.

Is your keyboard still messed up? You may have a "switchable" keyboard—one that works with different kinds of systems. Look on the underside of the keyboard and see whether there is a switch of any kind. On PC-compatible computers, the switch is often labeled like this:

←A   X→

What does the switch mean? When the switch is flipped to A, the keyboard thinks it is sending information to an IBM PC AT. When the switch is set to X, the keyboard is talking IBM PC XT language. If your switch is set wrong, the keyboard could do some pretty kooky things.

Demon-stration

Amaze your friends and coworkers. Join the millions of happy computer users who have survived the office-planning phase of their computer experiences.

1. Get a piece of graph paper (small squares).

2. Roughly measure out the square footage of your office space.

3. Don't forget to draw in the door and any other obstructions you can't put a desk in front of.

4. Use a yellow marker to indicate your primary light source.

5. Use penciled-in Xs to show electrical outlets.

6. Draw an arrow highlighting the phone jack.

7. Now draw in the desk where you want it. (Be sure to leave room for the chair.)

8. On top of the desk, draw the system unit. (Or beneath the desk, if you're using a tower unit and want to keep it off the desktop.) Be sure to put the unit close to both an electrical outlet and the phone jack.

9. Now add the monitor, the keyboard, and the mouse. (Remember to account for your right- or left-handedness.)

10. Draw in the printer (allowing for paper flow).

Erase as necessary. Redraw. Start over if you have to. Then, when you're finished, arrange everything, connect the cables, and get your boss to take you to lunch. You earned it.

Summary

The way in which you arrange your system has a lot to do with your comfort while you use it. If you spend countless hours analyzing your purchase, get it all home, and put the system somewhere where it's difficult to use, you've wasted considerable time and money. You need to have the system you want in the place that you want it. Computer equipment can be bulky and hard to organize—especially if you've got many different wires stretching to different parts of your office. Take some time to get it the way you envision it before you start computing. Your comfort zone will help reduce your anxiety even before you begin.

Exorcises

1. True or false: Computer components are the little things inside your computer that allow it to run.

2. What should you do before you unbox your system?

3. Name three considerations for placing the system unit.

4. Why is lighting important?

5. True or false: Right-handed and left-handed systems should be set up the same way.

7th Encounter

Turning the Computer On— and Off

Goal

To give that monster LIFE!

What You Will Need

Your system, arranged the way you want it, with cables connected and plugged in.

Terms of Enfearment

on/off switch	cold boot
warm boot	self-test
reset	desktop
power down	Finder

Briefing

We're almost up to the moment of truth. Will it work or won't it? Assuming that you've set up your system the way you want it (even if you *don't* want it), given yourself plenty of room to work, and plugged everything in, you're ready to send an electrical charge of life through your PC or Macintosh.

Getting Ready To Flip the Switch

Before you power that computer up for the first time, take a second and make sure that all your bases are covered:

- Is the monitor plugged securely into the system unit?

- Is the keyboard plugged into the system unit? What about the mouse?

- Are all the thumbscrews tight?

- Have you taken the cardboard protectors out of the disk drives? (Usually only 5.25-inch drives have these protectors. They keep the inside of the drive from being damaged during shipping.)

- Look at your monitor. Is there a separate power switch for the monitor, or will the entire system come on when you flip the switch on the system unit?

- Are all the power cords plugged in?

- If your PC does not have a hard disk, take the DOS boot disk, place it in drive A, and close the drive door.

Which drive is which? If you have two, how do you know which is A and which is B? Generally, drive A is the top drive, and drive B is the bottom. Drive C is the name given to the hard disk. If your disk drives are side by side, A is usually on the left, and B is ordinarily on the right.

Power On!

All right, hold on to your hat. Reach around to the side (or the back, on Mac Classics) of the computer and flip that power switch.

> Actually, that on/off switch could be anywhere. PS/1s have the switch in front; so do PS/2s. PC clones may have the switch on the right side or the front. Others are on the back. Look around. You'll find it.

Lights should flash. The monitor may (or may not) blink into life. You may hear a beep or two while your system runs through a couple of *self-tests* (checks to make sure that everything is working properly).

If your monitor did not come on, look for the power button along the bottom, on the side, or in the back of the monitor. Push the button or flip the switch. You should hear a quiet crackling and then see some sort of screen display.

The PC Lives

If everything worked the way it should, your PC grunted a few times, displayed a message something like

```
System initializing
```

and scrolled a few lines of something on the screen so fast you couldn't read it. Depending on the version of DOS you are using (remember DOS? That's Disk Operating System), your computer may ask you to enter the date and time. The date prompt looks like this:

```
Current date is Fri 12-17-1993

Enter new date (mm-dd-yy):
```

Take a look at the date. If it's not correct, type the new date by typing the numeric month (like 03, for March), the day, and the year. Then press the Enter key (the big key to the right of the alphabetic part of your keyboard). The computer then changes the date to the one you entered.

You can change the time the same way (see fig. 7.1). Look at the offering the computer shows you; type the correct time, and press Enter.

Figure 7.1
*Entering the date
and time.*

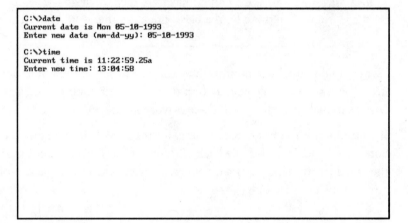

```
C:\>date
Current date is Mon 05-10-1993
Enter new date (mm-dd-yy): 05-10-1993

C:\>time
Current time is 11:22:59.25a
Enter new time: 13:04:58
```

How does the computer know? It may seem incredible that your computer knows what the date and time is. Many computers don't know, the first time they start up. Your computer has a battery-powered clock that keeps running even when the power to your system is turned off. The internal clock/calendar keeps track of the time and date and is powered by an ordinary battery.

After you enter the date and time, you find yourself staring blankly at something that looks like this:

```
C>
```

Not a real friendly screen, is it? Don't worry, you're not the only PC user who was ever put off by an initial impression. Things will get better.

A Mac is Born

Remember the Macintosh—the computer that wants to make things easy for new users? Startup is no exception.

Depending on the Macintosh you have, you may need to turn on a separate monitor. The Mac Classic includes the monitor built right in to the primary system unit; with that system, you can turn on the entire computer with one flip. Other Macs, however, like the Quadras and the Mac II family, require that you turn on separate power switches for the monitor and system unit.

After the initial beep, you see a Welcome to the Macintosh screen. Nice. The system is going through its self-tests to make sure that everything is working the way it should. After the test is completed satisfactorily, you see a smiling Mac. (Just a *bit* friendlier than the PC.)

The next thing you see is the computer's interpretation of a standard desktop. Actually, it looks like a big gray screen; but, as you work with the Mac, you'll see that it's meant to resemble a desktop (see fig. 7.2). In the upper right corner, you see a small box. This box is the on-screen representation of the hard disk in your machine.

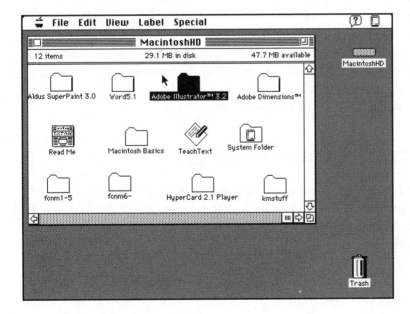

Figure 7.2
The Macintosh desktop.

If you are using a Mac that doesn't have a hard disk, you'll see instead a small disk icon, representing the boot disk you have in drive A.

Great, but What Does All This *Mean*?

Okay, you've survived the initial start-up phase. You know how to turn on your computer. Here are a few terms related to start-up you'll see used in other more jargony computer books:

Cold boot. A cold boot is what you just did—started the computer by flipping the power switch and sending electric current through its dead, cold, lifeless body.

Bootstrapping. This is a phrase only a techie could love, meant to refer to the process the computer goes through when you turn on the power.

Warm boot. A warm boot is what you do when you need to restart— or reset—your computer after you've been using it awhile. Rather than turning your system off and then on again, you can reset your computer in one of two ways: (1) by pressing the Reset button on the front of your computer or (2) by pressing and holding down the Ctrl, Alt, and Del keys and releasing them at the same time. (More about these important keys in the 8th Encounter.)

Preparing To Power Down

Well, that was exciting, wasn't it? Now all that remains is to shut everything off. Although we didn't do anything in this encounter, you should, as a general rule, run through a mental checklist each time you go to turn off your computer:

■ Have you saved your files?

■ Did you back up any important data?

■ Did you exit programs by using the Quit or Exit commands? (Don't just turn off power while a program is still displayed on the screen. Return to the DOS prompt or, for the Mac, to the desktop.)

Many business computer users ask themselves (and others) whether all the turning on and turning off that happens in a typical week is worth the wear and tear on the machinery. Often, the answer is No. Turning the system on and off repeatedly is hard on the hardware; however, leaving it on is a waste of energy. Computerists everywhere pooh-pooh the idea of wasted energy, claiming that it costs only cents a day to leave the computer on. But cost may not be our biggest problem.

A recent study has found, however, that most of the time the 30 million personal computers in this country are on, they are not being used. In fact, computers are currently responsible for more than five percent of all commercial electricity use in the United States. Researchers indicate that 40 percent of all computers are left on continually—including stretches of time over weekends and holidays.

The moral of this soapbox speech? Turn them off, when possible. And purchase energy-saving systems and screen-saving utilities if you're worried—not necessarily about cost, but about consumption.

Goodbye for Now

When you're ready to switch off your PC, turn off the other components first (printer, monitor—if it has a separate switch, and so on). Then, if you've exited out of any programs, reach around and turn off the switch. You'll hear the system clunking to a halt.

When you want to power down the Mac, the process is a little different. First, exit the program you were using and return to the desktop. Then open the Special menu (we explain how to use the mouse to open menus in the 9th Encounter) and choose the Shut Down command (see fig. 7.3). This prepares the Mac for the power outage. After you choose that command, a message appears:

```
You can now turn off the Macintosh safely
```

Figure 7.3
*Turning off the
Macintosh.*

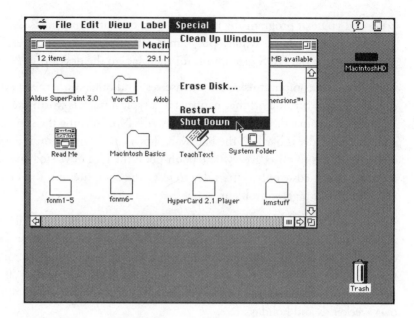

If you're using a single-unit Mac (like the Classic), you can turn off power by flipping the switch. If you have a Mac with separate components, turn each piece off independently.

They're Out To Get Us

Oh, but sometimes things don't work. What if—horror of horrors—you turn on the power and nothing happens?

Okay, Smartie—Nothing Happened

Perhaps it's stubbornness. See? Your PC senses your I-don't-want-to-use-this-blasted-computer vibe and is refusing to cooperate.

Or it could be karma. Perhaps something you did in a past life is coming back to haunt you.

Chances are, however, that your computer is refusing to work because something isn't connected properly. Check your surge protector. Is it turned on? Make sure that the plugs are all secure and everything goes into the wall somewhere.

Beeps and Blips

Other problems may pop up, too. Perhaps the computer starts, but it doesn't do what you want it to. On your PC, instead of the date and time prompts, you may see

```
Cannot find operating system.

Press any key to reboot.
```

If this happens, place a copy of your operating system disk in drive A and press any key. If the computer still doesn't display the DOS prompt or the date and time prompts, call your dealer. Fast.

Some PCs may be set up to display something different than the traditional DOS displays. The PS/1, for example, has a System Menu built right in so that you see a friendly opening screen from the minute you boot up.

Demon-strations

Boot Camp

Remember how to power up?

1. Make sure that everything is connected and plugged in.

2. If you don't have a hard disk, place your DOS (or system) disk in drive A.

3. Flip the main power switch.

4. Turn on the monitor, if necessary.

Honorable Discharge

Like anything else, with power downs, there's a right way and a wrong way. Doing it the wrong way might not bring disaster to your doorstep the very first time you do it, but sooner or later your laziness will come back to bite you. What's the lazy way? Reaching up and flipping the power switch while you still have programs running. The next time you try to run that program, it may go on strike.

To power down the right way, do the following:

1. Save any necessary files.

2. Exit the program.

3. Make sure that the DOS prompt or the Macintosh desktop is displayed.

4. On the Mac, open the Special menu and choose the Shut Down command.

5. Turn off the power.

Summary

Starting and shutting down your system are two of the easiest computer tasks you'll ever perform. Just use a little common sense—and put things back the way you found them—and these operations shouldn't give you any trouble. If your computer displays error messages or doesn't turn on no matter what you do, call your local computer technician for help.

Exorcises

1. What does the self-test do?

2. What should you check first if your computer does not start?

3. Match the following:

   _____ Warm boot   a. Powering up
   _____ Cold boot   b. Techie term for cold boot
   _____ Bootstrapping   c. Starting over without turning
                               power off

4. True or false: If you don't need to save any files, you can simply turn off power without exiting the program.

5. When should you call for help?

Tiptoe through the Keycaps

Goal

To help you find your way around the keyboard—whether you've purchased an IBM, a Mac, or some keyboard no one has ever heard of.

What You Will Need

A keyboard (no surprise there!).

Terms of Enfearment

alphanumeric	responsiveness
QWERTY keys	numeric keypad
cursor keypad	function keys
Enter key	Return key

Briefing

You're getting closer to actually using your computer—can you feel it? (Don't break out in a sweat; it's bad for your keyboard.) The keyboard is that often undervalued component that takes in everything you have to say and never sasses back. You can abuse it with heavy fingers typing at lightning speed, or you can toy with it using your hunt-and-peck, pointer-finger-only method of typing. It never complains.

What you may not know is that keyboards have different personalities. And there is no explaining this fact; two hundred keyboards can come from the same company, but many of them will have wildly different personalities. How do they vary? Read on.

Keyboard Personalities

Remember what they say about dog owners? After a while, they begin to look like their dogs. Keyboards tend to follow the same principle. That is not to say your keyboard will start to look like you, although it may end up having a personality like yours. Do you have a light touch when you type? Heavy fingers? You may type in short bursts or in a contemplative pattern, planning out your words before they appear on-screen. Sooner or later, your keyboard will reflect your particular typing style.

The Spring Touch

When you type, are your fingertips met by spongy, bouncy keys? You must be working with the Spring Touch. This keyboard, the cheerleader among keyboards, rises to meet your fingers as soon as the keys are pressed. In fact, you may find yourself double-typing characters because you're not sure that you've pushed them down far enough to register with the computer. Fast typists often like the Spring Touch because they can increase their already lightning-fast WPM rates by allowing their fingers to fly over the keys, barely touching the keytops.

> The keyboard's sensitivity (how hard you have to push the keys before the keyboard realizes a key has been pushed) is known as the *responsiveness* of the keyboard.

The Clackety Key

Most keyboard-computer combinations (like the early IBMs) have what's known as *key click*—an audible click that you hear each time you press a key. Some systems allow you to set the volume of the key click, from barely audible to really annoying. Again, touch typists like this feature because they can type that much faster without looking down. You may find that having the key click turned on too loudly or for too long (or being forced to listen to an officemate's loud key click) is a lot like having a yackety little sister that won't stop talking—you'll find yourself spending more and more time at the water cooler, trying to avoid her.

The Sticker

Some keyboards have nervous disorders. The obsessive Sticker becomes overly attached to a favorite letter (say, H) and repeats it over and over again after a single keypress. The word *hat*, for example, becomes *hhhhat*. Counseling won't help, but a trip to a computer technician equipped with alcohol and a cotton swab might.

The Invisible Eight

The malady my own keyboard suffers from is a different neurosis. I call it the Invisible Eight (because the first bout was with an 8 that went invisible all of a sudden). We've suffered several episodes together: first the 8, then R, then Y, and finally, L. After several hours (or days), the key comes back on its own. Advice? Have the thing serviced—and don't hesitate. One morning you could walk in your office and find the whole keyboard gone.

Keyboards aren't expensive, ranging from $80 to approximately $150. Trying to have a single key or two repaired, however, will be more expensive than replacing the entire keyboard. Better to have a spare keyboard, if possible (which may also frighten your keyboard into straightening up).

The Primo PC Keyboard

Chances are, you won't recognize the personality of your keyboard right off—you'll be trying to find what key is where and position your fingers accordingly. Luckily, most keyboards are somewhat similar in layout to typewriters; you won't have to hunt and peck (unless you were also a hunt-and-peck typist on a typewriter).

The first keyboard available for IBMs was the keyboard offered with the original IBM PC (see fig. 8.1). A great many people took shots at this keyboard: "It's too scrunched together" or "I keep missing the Enter key" were two of the big complaints. You have to give critics some credit—their fussing led IBM to introduce an improved keyboard with the PC AT, which led to the best IBM keyboard (which remains today's standard): the IBM Enhanced Keyboard (see fig. 8.2).

Figure 8.1
The original IBM PC keyboard.

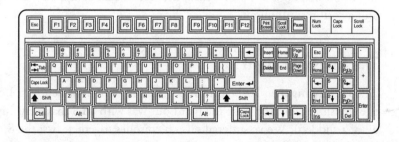

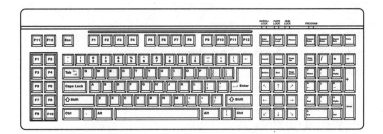

Figure 8.2
The IBM Enhanced Keyboard.

The Mighty Mac Keyboard

Like the PC, the Macintosh started out with an undersized, underpowered keyboard. It was little, like the original Mac, and wasn't to be taken seriously in a business environment. Today, the little Mac keyboard has grown into one of two more grown-up offerings: the Apple keyboard (see fig. 8.3), and the Apple Extended keyboard (see fig. 8.4).

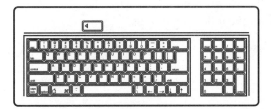

Figure 8.3
The Apple keyboard.

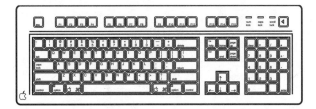

Figure 8.4
The Apple Extended keyboard.

Never one to follow the status quo for very long, Apple has recently introduced a startling new keyboard for those users worried about excessive keyboard use that might result in injury. (Yes, you heard right—*injury*.) Carpal-tunnel syndrome is a relatively new problem thrusting itself on unsuspecting computer users, and Apple has introduced a split keyboard (the two halves break apart, angling out as much as 30 degrees) that puts less pressure on your wrists by letting you type in a more natural way. The Apple Adjustable Keyboard is only slightly more expensive than the Extended, weighing in at $219 retail.

PC and Mac Keyboard Highlights

Some features are common to all keyboards, no matter what their family. These features can be divided into the following groups:

- QWERTY (or typewriter) keys
- Return or Enter key
- Cursor keys
- Function keys
- Numeric keypad
- Special keys

Qwerties

On any keyboard (IBM, Mac, Amiga, whatever), you'll find the standard set of alphanumeric keys. These keys are often called the *QWERTY* keys. Why? Because Q, W, E, R, T, and Y are the first six keys along the top left row of the keyboard. (You don't need a better reason than that, do you?)

Jargon alert. Alphanumeric refers to all the keys on the keyboard that are alphabetic, numeric, or symbolic (/, *, (, etc.).

You'll recognize the layout of the qwerties from the regular typewriter: three rows of letters, with a row of numbers above and symbols to the right. The spacebar stretches out below the bottom row of characters, easy to reach with either thumb.

No Deposit, No Return (or Enter)

Remember the carriage return on your old Smith-Corona? You pressed it at the end of each line of text to move the typeball down to the next line. On the PC and Macintosh keyboards, this key is the Enter or Return key (Enter on the PC, Return on the Mac).

Actually, the Macintosh has a Return key *and* an Enter key. The Return key is located along the right side of the QWERTY section of the keyboard, and the Enter key is in the bottom right corner of the numeric keypad, along the right side of the keyboard.

Pressing Return or Enter says "Do it!" to the computer. For example, suppose that you've entered the following DOS command, which lists all the files on a disk in drive A, at the DOS prompt:

```
DIR A:
```

When you press Enter, you tell the computer to execute the command you just typed. The computer responds by displaying a directory of all the files on the disk in drive A.

If you are using an application program—such as word processing, spread-sheet, or database—pressing Enter or Return may work similarly to a carriage return, by moving the cursor down one line.

Cursing Keys

One set of keys all keyboards have in common are the cursor keys. These keys appear on your keyboard marked like this:

Key Symbol	Key Name
→	right-arrow key
←	left-arrow key
↑	up-arrow key
↓	down-arrow key

Most popular keyboards today—like the Apple Extended and the IBM Enhanced—have two sets of cursor keys: one stand-alone set to the right of the QWERTY keys and another set that does double-duty as a numeric keypad, on the far right side of the keyboard (see fig. 8.5).

Figure 8.5
The cursor keys and the numeric keypad.

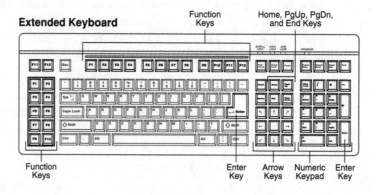

You can use either set for moving the cursor on the screen, but before you use the cursor keys on the numeric keypad, you must make sure that the keypad is not being used to enter numbers. How do you make sure? Check that the NumLock light (above the numeric keypad) is off; otherwise, when you press 4 (which also has the left-arrow symbol on it), you'll get a 4 on-screen instead of moving the cursor one place to the left.

The Function Key Family

Who started the idea of function keys? Someone, no doubt, who had little faith in the capabilities of the standard keyboard and thought we needed to heap still more buttons on these already-crowded components. Don't get me wrong; function keys *can* be functional. But I've yet to use any program—in more than 10 years' experience—in which I frequently need more than three of the function keys. So why 12? Or 15?

Function keys—labeled F1 through F12 (or F15, on some keyboards)—allow you to do things faster than you might if you didn't have them. Make sense? Suppose that you wanted to italicize a word. Using your word processor, you might be able to add a code that would make the word italic by pressing F7. If you didn't have that capability, you might have to choose two or three options from menus or dialog boxes in order to accomplish the same thing.

So function keys can save you keystrokes.

But on Macintosh keyboards, function keys are rarely used. Why? Because Mac software doesn't need them. Some keyboards allow you to program your own keys, which, at least initially, you won't be interested in trying. Suffice it to say that if you need the function keys, you know where to find them.

Special Keys

All around the QWERTY keys you see a variety of keys with different words and symbols. Some you might recognize from your typewriter days: Tab, Shift, and Caps Lock. Others, like Ctrl, Alt, and Esc, seem a bit cryptic. On the Mac, the Option and Control keys are new, as is the Command key, which shows the and the ⌘ symbols.

What do these keys mean, and when will you use them? Well, you already know the basics, but we'll rehash for you. Table 8.1 lists the special keys on the IBM Enhanced keyboard; table 8.2 explains the special keys on the Apple Extended keyboard.

Table 8.1. Special Keys on the IBM Enhanced Keyboard

Key	Does this:
Esc	Cancels an operation
Tab	Moves cursor forward
Caps Lock	Makes all typed letters capitals (when toggled on)
Shift	Used with letter or number keys to produce uppercase letters or symbols
Ctrl	Used with other keys to carry out commands or to select options
Alt	Used with other keys to carry out operations
Backspace	Moves the cursor one character to the left
Ins	Turns insert mode on so that any character typed will be inserted at the cursor position. (Pressing Ins again turns insert mode off, so any characters typed overwrite existing characters.)
Home	In most word processing applications, moves cursor to the beginning of the current line
PgUp	Scrolls the screen up one page
Del	Deletes highlighted information or character at the cursor position
End	In most word processing applications, moves cursor to the end of the current line
PgDn	Scrolls the screen down one page

Most of the special keys on the IBM Enhanced keyboard are also included on the Apple Extended keyboard. The exception is the Alt key (there are two Alts on the IBM keyboard), which is replaced with the Option key and the Command key on the Apple keyboard.

Table 8.2. Special Keys on the Apple Extended Keyboard

Key	Does this:
Esc	Cancels an operation
Option	Used with another key to select a command or option
Control	Used with other keys to carry out an operation
Command	Used in combination with other keys
Clear	Found on numeric keypad, clears number most recently typed

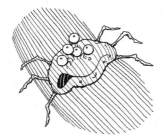

They're Out To Get Us

So what can go wrong with a keyboard? Not too much, fortunately.

Keyboards require some maintenance, like anything else, and perhaps a little extra care, if you want to keep them for any length of time. They don't get along with spilled cups of coffee. Paperclips wedged between the keys can wreak havoc among the characters. Dust, pet hair, and chocolate-chip cookie crumbs build up almost unnoticed until you've got a gummy paste that holds keys down even when you're not pressing them.

For best results, at least once a year, have the keyboard serviced. The tech will use some cotton swabs and some alcohol to clean around and perhaps under the keycaps, removing grease and grime and wax build-up. That will keep the component squeaky clean, at least until you knock over that can of Coke with your elbow!

Demon-strations

Pecking at the PC

Let's try a few sample typing episodes. Speed isn't important; getting familiar with the key layout is. Make sure that the computer is turned on; the DOS prompt C> should be displayed.

1. Type *Hi, Computer!* and press Enter. Did the computer answer you? (It should have said Bad command or file name, which means that you weren't speaking its language.)

2. Press Tab. What happened? (The cursor moves several spaces to the right.)

3. Practice typing a sample sentence and press Enter a couple of times.

4. Press and hold down the Ctrl key while you press B. Release both keys. On-screen, what you typed appears as ^B. Using two or more keys together is known as a *key combination*.

Mixing It Up with the Mac

There's not a lot you can do for typing practice when you're staring at the Mac desktop. Turn the computer off, and type a sentence or two. Press

Return to get a feel for the key. You also can practice key combinations like Command-P, Shift-T, and Option-B.

Summary

The keyboard is an often undervalued piece of your computer equipment. Don't underestimate the importance of having a keyboard you get along with—one with keys that "feel" right, one with a key layout that makes sense to you. You'll be spending lots of time interacting with your computer through the keyboard, so finding one you like—and taking the time to get comfortable with it—will be time well spent.

Exorcises

1. Explain responsiveness and tell why it is important.

2. What criticisms were made of the original PC keyboard?

3. Which key is the Go key? On the PC? On the Mac?

4. Name the six different key groups on your keyboard.

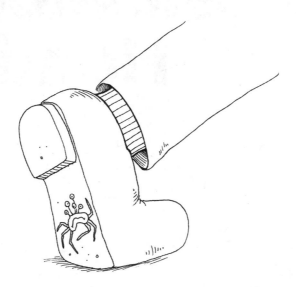

LITE
CHEEZ

Basic Mouse-Handling

Goal

To help you learn what a mouse is, to try it out, and to find out about basic rodent care.

What You Will Need

Your computer turned on and your basic mouse already connected to the system.

Terms of Enfearment

mouse	mouse ball
mouse buttons	mouse cable
pointing	clicking
double-clicking	dragging
pointer	

Briefing

Okay, your computer is on, and you've explored the basics of your keyboard. There's another computer tool you need to know about, one Macintosh users cannot do without, one that's been creeping into hearts of even the hardest-nosed PC enthusiasts: the mouse.

The mouse first appeared along with the Macintosh in early 1984. For the first time, computer users were given an option to the rather tedious (and confusing) method of working with programs by using the keyboard alone. The mouse was an instant success when users saw how simple it was to use; computering would never be the same.

Gradually, the popularity of the mouse forced PC software developers to reconsider their stance on mouseless programs. A few programs became available with "mouse support," enabling users to purchase a mouse and to use it with the program if they desired. The majority of PC users, however, remained true to their keyboard-only upbringing.

Today, the mouse is still a part of the Mac package: buy a Mac, get a mouse. Rarely do you see PC systems sold as a unit that includes a mouse. (The IBM PS/1 is an exception.) However, you can pick up a mouse for a nominal cost (I paid $29 for the one I'm using now!) or you can buy a top-of-the-line Microsoft mouse for somewhere around $129. With the explosion of mouse-supported software in the PC realm (thanks to Microsoft Windows), a mouse is a wise investment.

Rodents 101

Welcome, class. Gather around so you easily can see easily while we dissect this little rodent before us. First, however, let's go over a few definitions:

A mouse is technically called a *pointing device* (see fig. 9.1). The mouse is a small piece of equipment that fits comfortably beneath your hand (*which* hand depends on whether you are right- or left-handed). The mouse allows you to point to things on a computer screen and to click a mouse button to select the item you were pointing to. This allows you to bypass typing cryptic commands at an unfriendly DOS prompt in order to select commands and run programs.

Figure 9.1
Your basic, run-of-the-mill mouse.

Two kinds of mice are available for PCs: bus mice and serial mice. These two mice work the same way. The only difference between them is the way they are connected to your computer (see fig. 9.2). If you are using a *bus mouse*, the mouse is connected through an opening in the back of your computer to a board that is plugged into one of the expansion slots (remember those?). If you are using a *serial mouse*, the mouse is connected to the serial port in the back of your computer.

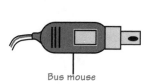
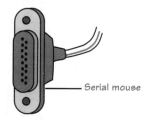

Figure 9.2
A bus mouse and serial mouse.

Serial mouse

Bus mouse

Which is better? That depends on the other items you want to attach to your computer. Either way, one of your resources is used by the mouse: an expansion slot or the serial port.

Jargon alert: The word *serial* refers to the way in which data travels through the port. You don't need to be concerned with this beyond understanding that a serial mouse is connected to the serial port. The serial port is probably labeled COM1 or COM2 on the back of your system.

How does the mouse work? Well, let's flip this little fellow over and take a look (see fig. 9.3). On the belly of the mouse, you see a round circle, inside which is a small, moveable black ball. You can easily move this ball with your finger. When you push the mouse (right-side-up) across the desktop, the ball rolls, pushing against one of four very sensitive electrodes inside the mouse. These movement sensors send information to your computer and to the program you're using, and the arrow on-screen that represents the mouse position (called the *mouse pointer*) is moved to match the mouse's movement on the desktop (see fig. 9.4).

Figure 9.3
Underneath the mouse.

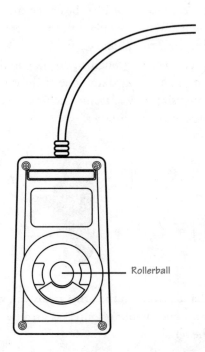

Rollerball

All this happens in a fraction of a second, so the mouse pointer on-screen appears to move the same instant your hand moves the mouse.

The only real difference between PC mice and the Macintosh variety is the number of buttons on top. The Mac mouse has only one button—that's all you'll ever need, working with Macintosh programs (see fig. 9.5). PC mice, however, may have two or three. The Microsoft mouse has two. The leftmost button is the one that is recognized in all mouse-supported programs, but different programs use the right button (or buttons) in different ways. That's always been a viable criticism of the PC world: lots of variety, but little consistency.

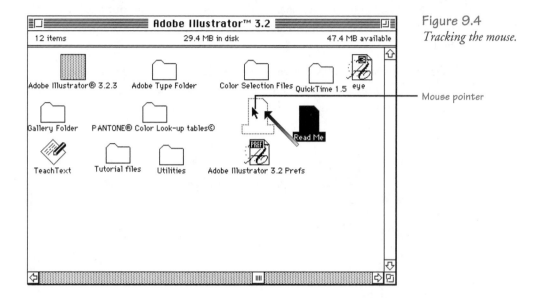

Figure 9.4
Tracking the mouse.

Mouse pointer

Figure 9.5
The Macintosh mouse.

Taming the Mouse

Now that you've had an up-close look at the mouse, are you ready for some mouse-wrangling? After mastering a few simple mouse techniques, you'll be ready to point and click with the best of them.

You are in for these mouse experiences:

- Moving and pointing the mouse
- Clicking and double-clicking the mouse buttons
- Dragging items

Moving the Mouse

Moving the mouse is as simple as moving your hand. You place your hand
on the mouse (so the round back of the mouse fits against your palm). Your
index finger should rest on the left mouse button (unless you are left-
handed).

Push the mouse one or two inches on your desktop. The pointer on-screen
moves as the mouse moves (see fig. 9.6). When you move the mouse so that
the pointer is positioned on something you want to select, you are doing
what's known as *pointing*.

Figure 9.6
Pointing the mouse.

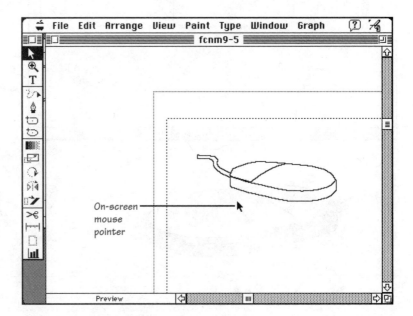

Pushing Your Mouse's Buttons

You select items and carry out commands by clicking the mouse button.
This is the mouse's version of the Go key (remember that from the 8th
Encounter?). A mouse click is technically a two-step process: press the mouse
button and then release the mouse button.

Some operations—like starting a program on the Mac—require that you double-click the mouse button. A double-click is simply—you guessed it— two quick clicks of the mouse button.

Dragging Items

Yet another technique allows you to select and move items on the screen. This process is known as dragging. To drag an item, you first point to it; then press and hold down the mouse button while moving the mouse. This drags the item in the direction you move the mouse (see fig. 9.7). When the item is in the desired location, release the mouse button to let go of the item.

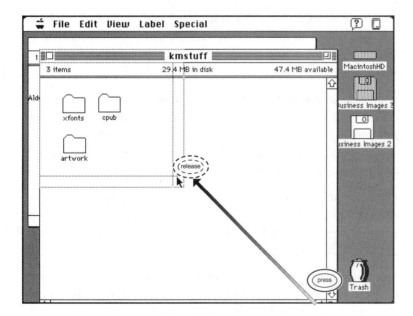

Figure 9.7
Dragging with the mouse.

The House Mouse and the Office Mouse

You remember the city mouse and the country mouse? Well, depending on your climate, you may find that your mouse acts differently in the home or office. The biggest differences between the two are the hazards in each environment.

If you have an office mouse, watch out for coffee spills, stray pieces of Post-It notes or disk labels, cigarette ashes (does anybody smoke in the office anymore?), and any other gummy or foreign substance that could get up inside the mouse.

If you have a house mouse, the perils are increased. Particularly if you have a set of computer-literate kids, you may find your mouse maligned with gummy bear remains, sand from the sandbox, spilled Squeeze-Its, pet hair, and heaven knows what else (sometimes it's better not to ask).

Mouse Cousins

We've been talking about the standard mouse as though that's the only kind there is. Not so. The type of mouse we've been discussing is known as the mechanical mouse. You may also see ads (or actually get your hand on) an *optical mouse* or a high-res mouse.

Remember the sensors inside your mouse's belly? And that ominous-looking black ball? The optical mouse does away with that mechanical technology in favor of laser optics. You put the optical mouse on a special pad that has a wire grid inside; when you move the mouse, the mouse "sees" where it's going by bouncing a light beam off the wire grid.

A *high-res* mouse is just an extremely sensitive mouse. (He cries every time he watches a Tom and Jerry cartoon.) The high-res mouse is very responsive, even to the tiniest movement. If you've got the hiccups, your mouse pointer may be jumping all over the screen.

Another cousin that is not a mouse is the *trackball.* The Macintosh PowerBook is the first big-name computer to incorporate the trackball in the machine. A trackball works on the same basic principle as the mouse; the small ball moves, touching sensors that send movement information to the computer. However, instead of moving the entire device, you move only the ball, rolling it with your thumb or index finger (see fig. 9.8).

Clip-on trackballs have been available for laptops and notebook computers for some time, but the Macintosh is the first to build the device into the system. A trackball is great for users who need this kind of computing power on-the-go. You obviously can't use a mouse when you're computing in your lap (or on a tiny airline tray) at 30,000 feet; a trackball stays put and lets you get mouse power from your favorite mouse-supported programs.

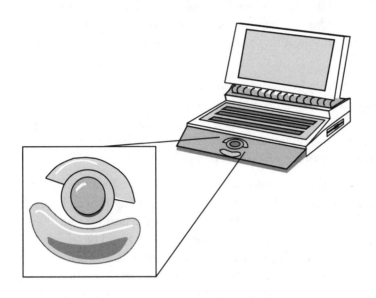

Figure 9.8
The Macintosh PowerBook trackball.

They're Out To Get Us

What can happen to a mouse?

Sticky Paws. The most common malady to afflict both home mice and office mice is sticky feet. Your mouse may be working fine one minute and then—oops—it slides across the desktop, not tracking anything.

Ball Warts. Sounds painful, doesn't it? Not too long ago, my mouse seemed to be limping across the desktop. I'd roll it to the right, and it would be fine; I'd roll it to the left, and—bump—I'd feel it roll over something. I picked it up and looked—nothing there. The mouse pointer would jump half way up the screen each time I hit that bump. Finally, I took off the ball cover and peered inside. There it was. A tiny piece of red Lifesaver had attached itself to the mouse ball.

Dead Mouse. Mice seem to have incredibly long life-spans and appear, for all practical purposes, to be hardy and easy to maintain. When might a mouse go belly up? When the mouse cable gets disconnected, for one thing. If your mouse is not responding to movement, check the back of your computer to make sure that everything is plugged in tightly.

Dead Mouse, Part Two. You could also have a software problem that makes your mouse play dead. (It's not *really* dead—it's just playing.) If you have a serial mouse and work with a program that uses the serial port for something else (for example, a communications program), that port could be "blocked" with electronic by-products. If you've checked the connections, made sure that the mouse cable is tight, and the mouse still doesn't work, try turning everything off, waiting 15 seconds, and turning things on again. If you still get no pulse, call 911.

Demon-strations

Let's put that little guy to work. If you are working with a Mac, you've got no problem—there's the mouse and the mouse pointer, ready to get going. If you're working with a PC, you'll need to start up a program that uses the mouse (something like Microsoft Windows). We haven't covered how to start a program yet (that's the 16th Encounter), but you may want to skip ahead and go through it now, so you can follow along.

Mouse Olympics

1. Place your hand on the mouse and move the mouse to the menu bar (see fig. 9.9).

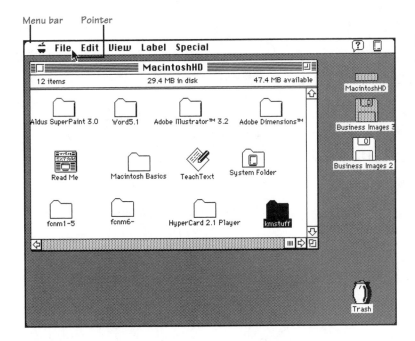

Figure 9.9
Pointing to the menu bar.

2. Position the mouse on one of the menu names.

3. Click the mouse button. The menu opens (see fig. 9.10).

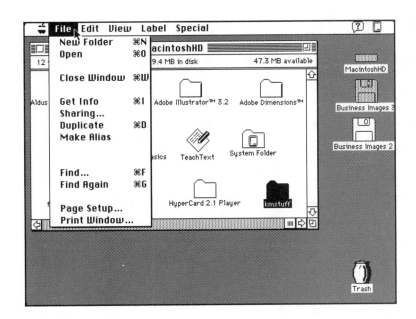

Figure 9.10
Using the mouse to open a menu.

4. Move the mouse pointer off the menu area and click. The menu closes.

Working-Class Mouse

1. On the Mac desktop or in the Windows Program Manager, move the mouse pointer to an icon in a window.

2. Press and hold down the mouse button.

3. Drag the item to a new location in the same window.

4. When the item is in the new location, release the mouse button.

Summary

The mouse is an integral part of Macintosh applications and is becoming a more popular part of PC programs all the time. Using the mouse is simple; just point and click, double-click, or drag. Like an extension of your own hand, the mouse lets you act quickly, selecting items on-screen, carrying out commands, and manipulating objects (and other fun stuff).

Exorcises

1. Which machine introduced the mouse?

2. Which PC is sold with a mouse included?

3. What kinds of mice are available?

4. Name five mouse actions.

5. When you move an item from one part of the screen to another, you use the technique known as _____.

A Look Inside
the Computer

Goal

To find out what's going on in there. Why? So you won't ever have to think about it again!

What You Will Need

A few minutes to kill.

Terms of Enfearment

system unit	CPU
RAM	ROM
motherboard	expansion slots
data bus	binary
bit	byte
kilobyte	megabyte

Briefing

Everything you never wanted to know about computers. Next on Geraldo.

Inside that system unit lurks some mysterious stuff. If you're lucky, you'll never see it. There will never be a reason for you—or anyone within sight—to pop the cover off the unit and do some major surgery.

But things break and wear out, and sometimes, just quit. In case one or all of those things happen, you should know a little something about the internal workings of your computer.

Mensa, Here I Come: The CPU

You've probably heard the rumors: Deep inside that computer is a single chip that does all the computer's thinking. That chip is called the *CPU* or the *microprocessor*. (CPU stands for central processing unit.) The small chip, which is probably about the size of your thumbnail, is a little black rectangle with metal legs on each side (see fig. 10.1). The chip is plugged into a socket on your computer's motherboard.

Figure 10.1
A microprocessor.

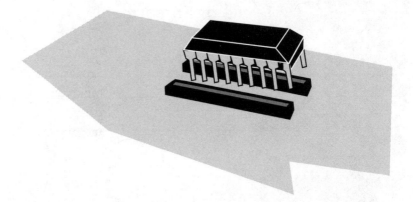

As you learned in the 3rd Encounter, PCs have microprocessors from the Intel 80X86 family. Older systems have the 80286 or 80386; today's standard (but tomorrow's bargain) is the 80486. The 80586 is on the horizon. The Macintosh uses a microprocessor from Motorola. These are numbered 68000, 68030, and 68040.

The microprocessor contains instructions that are responsible for the processing of all information. This information is burned onto the chip when it is manufactured. What does this mean to your computer? That every bit of information that comes in from the keyboard, mouse, modem, whatever must go first to the CPU and then be routed to its destination. As you can imagine, there's lots of data—in the form of electrical bits—running along the data paths in your machine.

Captain! We've Hit the Motherboard!

As we said, the microprocessor is plugged into the *motherboard*. This is a catchy word for the main board in your computer system. Data paths, capacitors (don't worry about them), and a variety of other interesting looking electronic things decorate the data highways. The CPU is seated there. Expansion slots (we'll explain in a moment) live there. Your computer's memory is situated there. Having to replace a motherboard, as you might expect, is a pretty costly and labor-intensive deal. Chances are, you'll never even know it's in there.

Sheepish about RAM?

RAM is an acronym for random-access memory, the set of memory chips in your computer (on the motherboard) that store the programs and data you work with in the current work session. RAM stores information only temporarily, while you or your computer is working with it. When you turn off power to your system, anything stored in RAM disappears (see fig. 10.2).

The earliest PCs had only 64K (that's kilobytes) of RAM. Today's systems are equipped with 2M (that's megabytes) or higher, much higher. Computers sold today often can be expanded to store as much as 32M (*remember Megabytes?*).

Figure 10.2
*RAM stores data
temporarily.*

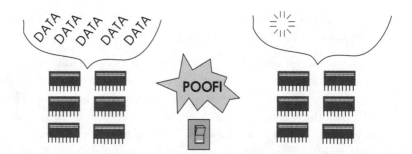

If you're unsure of how much RAM your system has, there's an easy way to check. If you're using the Macintosh, open the Apple menu and choose About the Finder. If you're using a PC armed with DOS 5.0 or later, type *MEM* at the DOS prompt and press Enter.

How will RAM affect you? Some programs require an enormous amount of RAM in order to work properly. If you don't have enough RAM, some programs will lock up, crash, or otherwise conk out. Other programs can get by on a minimum amount of RAM. Check with the programs you plan to use (and with your system's documentation) before trying a program that needs a hefty amount of RAM.

ROM Sleep

ROM is an acronym for read-only memory. This type of memory is also stored on chips plugged into the motherboard. ROM is not memory that will be used by your programs and data, like RAM; rather, ROM stores information your computer needs for its own internal processing. ROM chips have instructions burned on them that cannot be erased or modified. Those instructions are, truly, set in stone.

Every computer has its share of ROM, and no computer needs a ROM upgrade. You've got what you've got, and that's enough.

Pardon Our Dust: Room for Expansion

Also inside the system unit are expansion slots (part of the motherboard, again). These slots are available spaces for plug-in cards you will add when you build onto your system (see fig. 10.3). Your monitor, for example, runs because there is a video card plugged into one of the expansion slots on the motherboard. The video card interprets the data sent to it by the microprocessor and creates the display you see on-screen. (For more about video cards and monitors, see the 12th Encounter.)

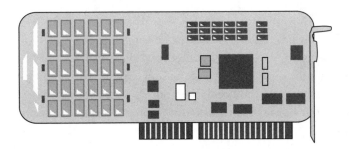

Figure 10.3
A board is added to the motherboard through the use of an expansion slot.

Other items you might plug into expansion slots include a printer card, a mouse card, a memory expansion card (which gives your system more RAM), or a sound board. Then you can add a printer, mouse, etc., by plugging the item into the connector that sticks out the back of the computer.

Powerful Stuff!

Let's not overlook that square metal box located in the back corner of your system unit (see fig. 10.4). If the power were on—and if you're actually looking at the power supply with the system unit cover off, the power should *not* be on—the small box would be humming a monotone tune. That box is the piece that supplies the power for your computer system. Inside that box is also a cooling fan that keeps that hot little motor from burning things up.

Figure 10.4
*The omnipotent
power supply.*

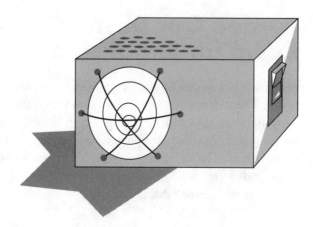

In most cases, you'll never have to deal with a power supply, unless one dies on you, which rarely happens. Sometimes, computer addicts want to upgrade their power supplies—that is, replace the standard one with a more powerful one—but these are also the people who put Porsche engines on riding lawn mowers. Your power supply, just as it is, should be good enough for your daily use.

Jargon Overload

Some things in computerdom are impossible to talk about without sinking to the level of computer jargon. We'd like to think it's avoidable, but, when push comes to shove, too many things blinked into consciousness because of the computer age, and so they were named by the computer age. Things like bytes, bits, and nibbles did not exist before the first computer came along and some scientist in a white coat (no doubt with at least ten degrees in computer science from Major Universities) said "Hey! We need a name for this whozits." He was answered by a similarly educated genius, who said "I know—let's call it a *nibble*!"

Binary? What's Binary?

Remember that year in math class when you were studying different counting systems? (I don't either.) We humans, of course, count on our fingers, which gives us the Base 10 method of counting. We count zero to nine; then we essentially start over on a second ten, which goes from 10 to 19. Then the third ten ranges from 20 to 29. You get the idea.

If we had five of something, we might have instead started our numbering system based on five. Maybe we'd count like this: 0, 1, 2, 3, 4, 10, 11, 12, 13, 14, 20, 21, 22, 23, 24! Well, thank goodness we don't have to do *that.*

Binary is a system that counts by twos. (We must have looked down and used our feet for that one.) Zero and one—that's all you have to work with. Your computer uses the binary counting system to keep track of the electronic pulses that are at the essence of all your computer work. This binary system represents the two states of these electronic pulses: they're either on (1) or off (0).

All information in your computer is sent from chip to chip, card to card, and item to item in binary form. Each piece of data is actually written in binary form, something like this:

```
1010 0011
```

This piece of data goes on its journey through the computer. The processor reads the information as "First pulse on, second pulse off, third and fourth pulses on!" and so on.

Kudos and Bits

Each place that is marked by a 0 or 1 is called a *binary digit,* which is shortened to *bit.* A bit of information is a single electronic pulse (either on or off). One bit isn't going to tell the computer much of anything, so the bits are grouped together. Much like a single letter doesn't communicate anything to you, but when you put the letters together to form a word, you can get my meaning.

Bytes

One standard established long ago to refer to this grouping of information is a *byte* (pronounced "bite"). A byte is eight bits, like this:

```
0001 1101
```

In its binary form, a byte can communicate up to 256 different values, from 0 to 256. Zero is 0000 0000 (all off), and 256 is 1111 1111 (all on). In human terms, one byte of information is roughly equivalent to one word.

This means that although a byte is much larger than a bit, it still is incapable of telling us much. To use a real-world analogy, one byte of information could be compared to one flea on your average-sized dog (see fig. 10.5). If you don't know precisely where it is, you're not going to find it. (A bit would be one leg of the flea on the average-sized dog.)

Figure 10.5
A byte is to your computer as a flea is to a dog.

Bytes are written, as shown, in two sections of four bits each. Each group, which represents half a byte is called a *nibble*. Somewhere in the world, there is a very proud computer techie, polishing his pocket protector and saying "See? And they said we didn't have a sense of humor!" (The jury is still out.)

Kilobytes

So data is stored and transmitted in bytes of information. Many, many bytes of information are used to communicate a single instruction to your computer. The storage space your computer has is explained in terms of how many bytes of information it can hold.

Remember RAM? (The chips inside your computer that temporarily store the programs and data you are working with.) Early computers had only 64K of RAM. The K stands for *kilobytes,* which is 1,024 bytes of information. (Some people say a kilobyte is 1,000 bytes, but that's a 24-byte understatement.) When you begin to work with files, you'll be able to tell how large the file is (how much memory it needs) because the file size will be displayed in kilobytes.

If a bit is the leg of a flea and if a byte is one flea on the average-sized dog, a kilobyte is comparable to having the poor fellow immersed in fleas (see fig. 10.6). From head to foot, that rascal is a wandering ecosystem for more than a thousand fleas. (Better check your ankles.)

Figure 10.6
*From **byte** to kilobyte.*

Megabytes

Today's computers are equipped with 2M (or more) of RAM. The M is for *megabytes*. As you may know, mega means million, so megabytes tells you how many *millions* of bytes your computer can store. The exact number of bytes in one megabyte is 1,048,576. *Now* we're talking.

Megabytes are used to explain how much information you can store on your hard disk, as well. Early hard disks stored only 10M—huge, we thought, at the time—but today's computers are equipped with 120M, 210M, or larger hard disks.

Ready for an analogy upgrade? Okay, with a kilobyte, the dog was covered in fleas. A megabyte is one thousand times worse, so now your whole house is full of fleas (see fig. 10.7). (And that's a pretty big house, too.)

Figure 10.7

A megabyte is a thousand kilobytes.

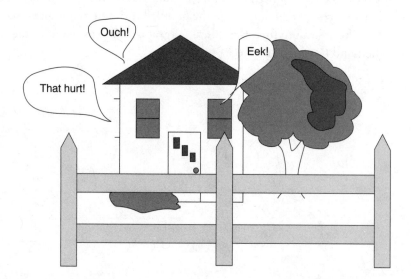

Gigabytes

Onward and upward. Are we happy with today's high end? No, we're not. We need more storage. And more memory. Already we're seeing enormous storage capacities, with the *gigabyte* roughly equivalent to one billion bytes of information (that's 1,000 megabytes). The gigabyte technically is 1,073,741,824 bytes.

Time for the Queen Mother. Not only does your dog, your house, your
family, your car, and your mother-in-law have fleas, but now your entire
neighborhood—every house, every inch—is covered in fleas (see fig. 10.8).
Needless to say, your neighbors aren't real fond of you.

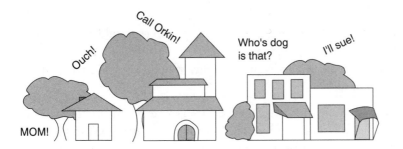

Figure 10.8
*A gigabyte is one
thousand megabytes.*

Hmmm. As you can see, a gigabyte is one whopping amount of storage
space.

They're Out To Get Us

Even though the system unit houses some highly technical and sophisticated pieces of equipment, there isn't much—short of a power surge—that can do too much damage.

The most common ailment might be a memory chip that suddenly goes bad. (When chips go bad. Next, on Geraldo.) How will you know? You'll see a strange message on-screen, and your computer won't go any further. You may hear a beep, too.

Anytime you see an error message on the screen, write down exactly what the message says and ask someone about it. Your system may not fail today or even tomorrow, but something is wrong or in the process of going wrong, or that error wouldn't have appeared in the first place.

As mentioned earlier, power supplies can go out; fans can break down; the motherboard can receive a jolt of electricity and fry herself up. (Get out the checkbook.)

For now, just keep unfriendly elements—water, Coke, coffee, smoke, dust, and so on—as far away from the system unit as possible.

Summary

From a small chip inside your computer comes all the processing necessary to perform an almost unlimited number of tasks. Other things help, of course; RAM gives your system the memory it needs to store programs and data; ROM tells your system how to start and run itself; expansion slots allow you to (eventually) add on as necessary.

Exorcises

1. Match the following with their descriptions:

    _____ Computer "brain"   a. RAM

    _____ Room to grow   b. ROM

    _____ Memory   c. Motherboard

    _____ Electric current   d. Microprocessor

    _____ Place CPU is socketed   e. Power supply

    _____ Burned-on instructions   f. Expansion slots

2. What is a bit?

3. List the six measurements of memory in order (from smallest to largest):

    _____   Megabyte

    _____   Bit

    _____   Nibble

    _____   Gigabyte

    _____   Byte

    _____   Kilobyte

11th Encounter

What's the Big Deal about Disk Drives and Storage Space?

Goal

To help you find out how programs and files are stored.

What You Will Need

Access to either a 5.25-inch or 3.5-inch drive (or both) and the disks to go with them.

Terms of Enfearment

disk drives	hard disk
floppies	fixed disk
minifloppy	microfloppy
reading data	writing data
CD-ROM drive	secondary storage device
density	

Briefing

The computer wouldn't save you much time if you had to re-enter all the information you needed every time you fired the system up. Storage is a supremely important issue. How you store the information you work with on your computer—whether you store that data on floppy disks or on a hard disk—is more a matter of convenience and personal choice. The fact that you do save your information is the most important issue.

Why Storage Space Isn't RAM

People often confuse the terms *storage space* and *RAM*. What's the difference? RAM, as you may remember from the 10th Encounter, is the segment of memory that stores the programs and data you work with during a current work session. Temporarily. When you turn the power off, everything in RAM is erased. The next time you start your computer and begin working with a program, that program is loaded into RAM.

Storage space, on the other hand, keeps your programs and data until you delete them. When you type the necessary command to start a program (or use the mouse to click on the appropriate picture, or icon), the computer knows to search the storage device to find the program you want. The program is then loaded into RAM, ready for you to use. Figure 11.1 illustrates the difference between RAM and storage space.

Figure 11.1
RAM and storage differences.

Temporary Storage of Programs and Data

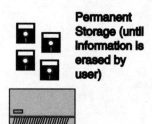

Permanent Storage (until information is erased by user)

When you save a file, the information is written out to a spot in storage. Before you save the file, it exists only in RAM, which means that if power is cut off, that file is history. For that reason, most people don't rely on RAM to store their files as they work on them; they save the file every 15 minutes or so. (You never know when someone is going to take a trip over the power cord.)

The bottom line? Information in RAM disappears as soon as power shuts off. Data in storage doesn't.

Storage Types

With the first personal computers, there was only one type of storage device available. Today, we've got several options for the way we store our data. Some are practical for everyday use, but others are better for that occasional jaunt down resource lane.

The most widely used method of storage is the floppy disk (see fig. 11.2). Disks store programs and data; you insert the disk into the drive, and the computer loads the information from the disk into RAM. When you save the file you are working on, the program places the most current copy of the file on the disk. When you purchase a program, the program comes to you on either 5.25- or 3.5-inch disks.

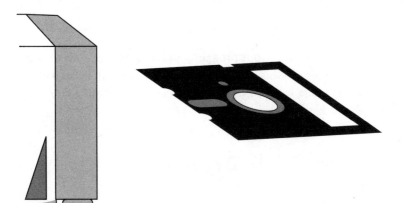

Figure 11.2
Everybody uses floppy disks.

Hard disks are storage devices that let you store large volumes of information without inserting anything into anything (the hard disk is enclosed in a drive case). The hard disk is usually housed inside the system unit of your computer, with the only thing showing being the hard disk access light that tells you when the computer is reading something from the hard drive. External—or out-of-system-unit—hard drives are also available; you plug these into one of the expansion ports in the back of your machine (remember those?).

CD-ROM drives allow you to read huge amounts of information from a CD (yes, they look just like musical CDs), but, as yet, the technology isn't there to let you write to the CDs. CDs are popular for educational software and reference libraries or for incredible volumes of work (like the Bible). You can read information from a CD in order to incorporate the information in a report, play a game, or use clip art graphics, but you cannot store your own information on the CD.

One main consideration that sets these storage devices apart is their speed. Floppy disks are relatively slow, at least by hard disk standards. Hard disks can retrieve files, save information, and write data much faster than floppy disk drives. The time it takes a CD-ROM drive to find information is remarkably faster even than hard disk access time; however, the CD-ROM is unable to write information to the CD for later use.

Tape backup units can store all your programs and data on tape, but they are used as secondary storage devices. That is, you don't work with them daily to load programs and data into RAM; you use them only to keep a safe backup copy of your hard disk contents.

The Dirt on Disk Drives

Disk drives were the primo storage device for the early PCs. There just wasn't anywhere else to put your data. The original IBM PC had one 5.25-inch disk drive.

Disk drives work by reading information from or writing information to the surface of a disk that is inserted in the drive slot. Recording heads read and write the information onto the exposed disk material. The drive also writes an index (called a *FAT*, or file allocation table) on the disk, so it knows where to find the information it has stored on that disk. Each disk has its own FAT that is updated every time a file is saved to the disk.

Floppy Swapping: 5.25-Inch Disks

The original disks used in those first PCs are still around—or, at least, some descendents of those same type of disks are in use today. 5.25-inch disks were the standard for both PCs and the early Apples, although a new size (3.5-inch) has become increasingly popular in the last few years.

Those early disks were—and are—referred to by a number of names. You might see *5.25-inch disk*, or *diskette*, or *floppy*. Some people get more technical and call it a minifloppy. For our purposes here, we call a disk a disk.

The 5.25-inch disk is a square, bendable piece of cardboard-covered plastic (see fig. 11.3). You can hurt, maim, or kill a floppy disk; the surface of the disk and the exposed plastic underneath make the disk vulnerable to all kinds of hazardous office or home wastes.

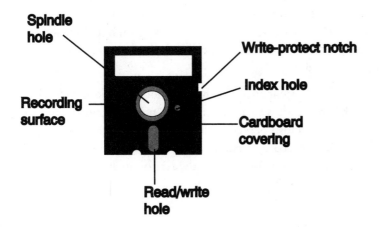

Spindle hole

Recording surface

Write-protect notch

Index hole

Cardboard covering

Read/write hole

Figure 11.3
Anatomy of a floppy disk.

When you slide the floppy disk into your 5.25-inch disk drive slot and close the drive doors, the disk drive seizes the disk, holds it in place, and spins it by inserting a spindle in the spindle hole. The drive uses the index hole to count the number of times the disk rotates (this allows the drive to locate the right place on the disk for storing or retrieving information). The drive then reads information from or writes information to the disk by using the read/write hole, which offers the largest amount of access to the recording surface.

> If the write-protect notch is covered by a piece of tape (or a write-protect tab), the drive will not be able to write information to the disk. Information can be retrieved *from* the disk, however.

When you release the door handle on the 5.25-inch drive, the spindle is removed, and the disk is pushed out so that you can easily grasp it. (Never open the drive door and remove a disk when the disk access light is on.)

The Toughskins: 3.5-Inch Disks

Another kind of disk has become popular in the last few years. Perhaps attributable to the Macintosh, the 3.5-inch disk is a sturdier, more reliable type of disk (see fig. 11.4). Other computers, like the early Sony, used the 3.5-inch disks long before IBM jumped on the bandwagon, but Macs were never manufactured with any other kind of drive. Right from the outset, the first Macs used 3.5-inch disks.

The 3.5-inch disk has a different anatomy than its more thin-skinned 5.25-inch cousin. The 3.5-inch disk is enclosed in plastic, making it much less vulnerable to elements like dust, pet hair, ashes, and melted Reeses Pieces. On the 5.25-inch disk, the recording surface of the disk is exposed through the read/write hole, but on the 3.5-inch disk, the read/write hole is covered with a piece of metal called a shutter.

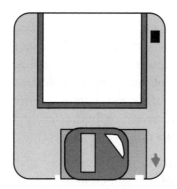

Figure 11.4
Anatomy of a 3.5-inch disk.

When you insert a 3.5-inch disk into a 3.5-inch drive, the process is different. First, you don't have to close the drive door; the 3.5-inch disk just pops into place. Then the spindle grabs the spindle hole (which is visible only on the back of the disk), and the drive slides the shutter open, revealing the read/write hole. The write-protect notch is not a notch at all but rather a switch; when you want to keep someone from writing on the disk, you just slide the little black tab to the write-protect position.

When you want to remove the 3.5-inch disk, you push the button on the drive; the disk is then pushed out so that you can reach it easily.

Most programs are offered on both 5.25-inch and 3.5-inch disks. Additionally, most new systems sold today have both 3.5-inch and 5.25-inch disk drives. This solves any problem you may have swapping floppies with co-workers or friends.

Are You Dense, or What?

What about densities? High density, low density, everywhere a den-sit-y!

Oh, but we're not done yet. Computer manufacturers had to make things more difficult for us by offering *two* kinds of 3.5-inch disks and two kinds of 5.25-inch disks. The kind of disk you use depends on the type of drive you have.

Confused? Read on.

First of all, think about the word dense. What does that mean, in normal speech? Dense, or density, is the word we use to describe the thickness, completeness, or volume of something. A really dense fog, for example, means that the fog was so thick you could cut it with a knife (figuratively, anyway). Density, when it relates to disks, refers to the thickness with which the data can be stored on a disk.

So a high-density disk means that you can store a large amount of data on the floppy disk. Low-density, then, means that you can store a smaller amount of data on the disk.

A high-density 5.25-inch disk can store up to 1.2M (that's megabytes, remember?) of data on one disk. A high-density 3.5-inch disk stores 1.44M.

> A new microfloppy disk is beginning to appear that is capable of storing a high-density amount of 2.88M. Unless your disk drive can recognize this type of disk, however, purchasing it would be useless.

A low-density 5.25-inch disk stores only 360K of data—not much by today's standards. The 3.5-inch counterpart stores a bit more: 720K.

> If you have a disk drive that works with high-density disks, you will be able to read information from and write information to low-density disks, as well. However, if you have a drive that requires low-density disks, you cannot work with high-density disks.

The Hard Facts about Hard Disks

It's a pretty safe bet that your computer has a hard drive. Computers just aren't sold today without them. The earliest PCs were equipped with only floppy drives, but that standard changed early in PC history, with the 10M hard drive of the first IBM PC XT.

11th Encounter ➤ What's the Big Deal about Disk Drives and Storage Space?

153

Today's hard disks are faster, better, and offer more than a hundred times the storage capacity. They are also—go figure—much less expensive.

And considering that the programs we use have gotten weightier, we need all the storage space we can get.

The hard disk works in much the same way as floppy disks; recording heads read information from and write information to the surface of the disk. The disk just happens to be enclosed in a case. The disk itself is not plastic but a hard platter (hence the name *hard disk*). You may also see the term *fixed disk* used to describe hard disks, because the disk is nonremovable and therefore "fixed" inside the unit.

Is Bigger Better?

In a word, yes. Best advice? Get the biggest hard disk you can afford. (Not biggest in the sense of physical dimensions; biggest in storage capacity.) You may be surprised at the amount of hard disk space you use.

At first, 40M seems like a lot. But when you add Microsoft Windows, Microsoft Word, and a few other popular programs, you've only got a few K left for data files. Not good enough.

120M is pretty standard these days. For many regular business applications—spreadsheets, report writing, light databases, etc.—that's probably good enough. For applications that take up quite a bit of storage, like really hefty databases, huge graphics files, and multimedia presentations, 210M or larger is the safer bet.

Stretching the Limits

It's possible to get more out of less, when it comes to your hard disk. Two different methods allow you to conserve space and fool yourself (and your computer) into thinking that you've got more room than you actually have.

Data compression programs—like Stuffit for the Mac and PKZIP for the PC—save files in more compressed chunks, thereby conserving space on the hard disk (or floppy, for that matter). The only problem is that you must expand the files again before you can use them. This is a small price to pay when disk space is at a premium.

Another type of utility uses a file-compression technique to "trick" the hard disk into thinking it has more room than it actually has. A program called Stacker is one example of this. You can literally double the size of your hard disk (from 120M to 240M) by using this or a similar program.

They're Out To Get Us

What can go wrong with storage devices? The devices themselves and the media on which the data is stored each have their own set of problems.

Disk Difficulties

Floppy disks—particularly the 5.25-inch variety—are notorious for going bad. ("My disk's gone bad." A user's story. Tomorrow, on Donahue.) You just used it; it seemed fine. Then you slide it back into the slot, enter a command, and!

```
Error reading drive A

Abort, Retry, Fail?
```

Disks get old. Disks get dirty. Disks get sticky and can gum up the read/write heads in your drive (much more serious).

For best results and the most reliability from your disks, choose a different "daily" disk at least every week; that is, if you read from and write to a disk on a daily basis, use a new disk every so often to reduce the chance of the disk wearing out.

Ahh-Choo!

Disks can also introduce a danger to your system; something unthinkable just a few years ago. With the advent of computer viruses, disks became suspect.

A virus may be something silly, with the result something as harmless as displaying the following message:

```
Legalize marijuana
```

Or the virus can be as serious as a cancer that slowly eats away all the most important files on your machine.

Today, you shouldn't accept a disk from someone you don't know (who knows where it's been?) and never use an inherited disk on your computer without running a virus-detection program on it first.

For more information on keeping your disks healthy, see the 19th Encounter.

Just in Case . . .

Hard disks tend to be much more reliable than their floppy relatives, but when they fail, they fail. Hard drives do crash, rendering you helpless and holding your data hostage. To protect yourself from the terror of a hard disk strike, back up (make copies of) your data and programs on a regular basis (like once a week). To prolong the life of your hard disk and protect your data, have the hard disk serviced every couple of months.

Demon-stration

Whether you're using a PC with a 5.25-inch drive or a system with a 3.5-inch drive, try out your disk drive by inserting and removing the disks. For 5.25-inch disks, the read/write hole should be facing up and away from you (toward the disk). For 3.5-inch disks, the shutter should be facing up and away from you.

Summary

Without storage devices, our computers would be useless. Although RAM stores programs and data during the current work session, as soon as you turn power off, that information is gone. In order to store programs and files and use them again another day, you need storage. And storage means disk drives and disks. Hard disks store large amounts of information and are housed permanently in a casing. Disks—5.25-inch or 3.5-inch—store information on plastic surfaces that your computer can read from or write to.

Exorcises

1. What's the difference between RAM and storage space?

2. Name four storage devices.

3. What are two major differences between disk drives and hard drives?

4. Match the storage capacities with the correct disk:

   5.25-inch _____ and _____   a. 720K

   3.5-inch _____ and ____   b. 360K

                                                    c. 1.44M

                                                    d. 1.2M

5. Name two things that can go wrong with floppy disks.

Here's Looking at You, Kid: Monitors

Goal

To help you understand the mysterious workings of your monitor and to learn about the features most important for display quality.

What You Will Need

Your computer hooked up and turned on and a monitor of some kind (quality isn't important. . .yet).

Terms of Enfearment

monochrome monitor	CGA
EGA	VGA
multisync monitor	resolution
graphics adapter	refresh rate
interlacing	

Briefing

Who wants to stare at a glaring, boring, shoddy-character, no-good-looking-graphics type of monitor all day long? Not me, certainly, and probably not you.

Something you're going to spend so much time with should, at least, make you mildly happy. The monitor is your liaison with the computer system. There's no getting around it; you'll be staring at the square face of your monitor all day, every day—or at least every minute you're working with your system.

And because the quantity of time is substantial, the quality of the display is essential. Squinting for eight hours a day gets really old really quickly. Hunching over in your seat so that you are looking straight into the monitor will give you the Boris Karloff look. Staring into a wavering screen will give you headaches.

This encounter will help you unravel the various rumors that surround the display of your computer. Do you need a monitor as large as a big screen TV? Is color the only way to go?

The Comfort Zone

One of the most important features of your monitor has nothing to do with whether it displays color or not. It may sound silly, but it's an important consideration: How do you feel when you're using it?

If you're not comfortable using your monitor because of your (and its) physical position, you'll be dissatisfied whether you're using a top-of-the-line $1,500 monitor or a clunky $298 blue light special. You shouldn't be scrunched over or stretching up in order to get the best vantage point; your monitor should be roughly eye level so that you can sit comfortably while working with it. If you're looking up, your neck will let you know; if you're looking down, your back will begin to ache.

> If your monitor is not eye-level and you can't fix that fact (by raising or lowering the monitor), you still have an option: Manufacturers sell monitor stands that have tilting or swiveling bases; you can then tilt the screen so that it looks down or up at you, even if you can't move the entire monitor.

Are you sitting close enough to the monitor that you can read text easily? One rather laid-back coworker set up his office around his favorite Lazy Boy; he'd push back in the recliner with the keyboard on his lap and do his programming stretched out almost horizontally. He couldn't understand why, when he was so relaxed at work, he continued to have terrible headaches. A trip to the optometrist told the story: eyestrain. Don't make your eyes work overtime—staring into a gleaming monitor for hours on end is hard enough.

> Two things: First, if you wear glasses, plan on getting eye exams more often (like every 10 months or so) if you are beginning to work with a monitor consistently. Many people find that text-intensive work leads to changes in eyesight. Also, especially at first, remember to take breaks every 30 minutes or so, even if you only look away and focus on something besides the monitor. This can help substantially reduce new-user eyestrain.

The Behind-the-Screen Scoop

How does a monitor work? Actually, the monitor is only one part of your computer's display system. It needs another item, called the *graphics card* (or sometimes, the *display adapter*), in order to show anything on the screen.

Remember the discussion of expansion slots? These slots are places on the motherboard that hold plug-in cards for other items you add to your computer system (like a printer, a mouse, or a monitor). The graphics card plugs into one of those slots on the motherboard (see fig. 12.1).

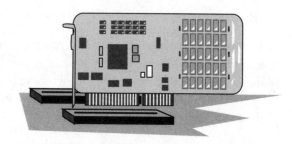

Figure 12.1
The graphics card plugs into the motherboard.

The graphics card works like a translator; it receives information from the microprocessor and turns it into information that can be displayed on the screen (see fig. 12.2). Without the card, your monitor wouldn't work. For example, when you type a letter, the information goes from the keyboard to the microprocessor; it then goes from the microprocessor to the graphics card. The card turns the signal into information that can be displayed on the screen, and the letter appears a fraction of a second after you typed it. All this happens so quickly that the individual character appears before you type the next one (which may or may not be miraculous, depending on your typing speed).

Figure 12.2
The display process.

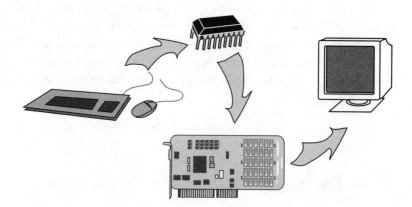

The graphics card sends the information to the monitor through a cable. The information is received by the monitor and fed to a device called an *electron gun*, which electronically paints the inside of the monitor, causing the phosphors on the inside of the screen to glow.

Sound confusing? Perhaps an analogy will help.

Imagine that you are about to paint a minibarn. You've purchased your paint, and now you're standing there, looking over your painting tools. Sure, you could use the roller, but—hey, this paint sprayer could be fun. You load the thing up with paint and, starting in the upper left corner of the barn side, you spray all the way to the right; then drop down a little and paint from right to left. You do this, all the way down the barn side.

Now you know what it feels like to be an electron gun.

New Year's Resolutions

One quality everyone is concerned about when it comes to monitors (and rightfully so) is screen *resolution*. The resolution of the display refers to the quality, or sharpness, of the display. A monitor with low-resolution has blocky text and grainy graphics. A high-resolution monitor offers well-formed characters and realistic-looking art.

The key to resolution is the size of the dots—called *pixels*—used to paint the screen. The smaller the dot, the more dots are used in the same amount of space. The bigger the dot, the fewer dots used, and the lower the resolution. Get it? This resolution issue applies to print as well as display quality (see fig. 12.3).

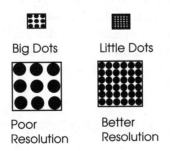

Figure 12.3
More dots make for better resolution.

If you were painting the barn and wanted to do a really good job, you would try to control the paint output so that the paint came out as a really fine spray; then you would paint slowly so the paint sprayed was very dense.

Early graphics cards and monitors displayed text and graphics at a low resolution. The first monitor/card combos were CGA (color graphics adapter) and EGA (enhanced graphics adapters). They used fewer dots than the screen resolutions offered today. Today, yesterday's top of the line is now the lowest standard, although the others are offshoots of the same technology:

Graphics card	Resolution
VGA	640 by 480
SuperVGA	800 by 600
Extended VGA	1024 by 768
Ultra VGA	1280 by 1024

When you're buying a monitor, concern yourself with these two issues regarding screen resolution:

■ **The dot pitch** (size of the dot). A dot pitch of .28mm to .31mm is within the realm of acceptable; anything larger will give you poorer resolution.

■ **The graphics card.** Don't purchase anything less than VGA (in fact, you may have trouble finding anything less than VGA) and purchase the highest quality you can afford. You may not need the highest standard, however, if you are working with a smaller monitor (why stuff 1280 by 1024 dots into a tiny monitor when a monitor capable of displaying 800 by 600 would work better?).

Ah, the Rate that Refreshes

But the barn will need another coat of paint, won't it? So after finishing the side, you move the sprayer back up to the top left again and start the whole process over.

The difference with the inside of your monitor is that the screen must be repainted again and again and again, into infinity, for as long as your monitor is turned on. After a fraction of a second, those glowing phosphors begin to fade, and the inside of the screen must be repainted.

The electron gun moves back and forth and from top to bottom. How quickly the gun moves is known as your monitor's *refresh rate*. The refresh rate can be a very important characteristic in the quality of your display; if the gun moves quickly enough, you never notice the phosphors fading in the top left corner of the screen. However, if the refresh rate is too slow, the screen will begin to fade before it is repainted, causing an annoying screen flicker (and sending you running for the aspirin bottle).

The rate at which the gun moves across the screen is known as the *horizontal refresh rate*; the rate for moving from top to bottom is the *vertical refresh rate* (see fig. 12.4). For best results and maximum monitor happiness, don't settle for a refresh rate of less than 72Hz (that's 72 screen paintings a second).

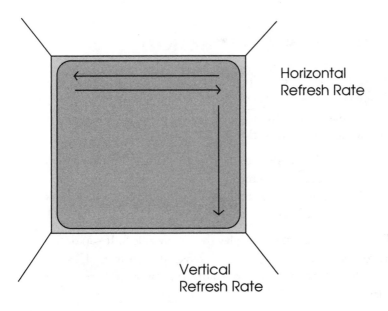

Figure 12.4
Rates of refreshment.

Horizontal
Refresh Rate

Vertical
Refresh Rate

Tying it Up: Interlacing

But what if you need to finish that blasted barn and you're really in a hurry? You might try skipping every other line, hoping that the effect blends together and that the barn still looks good.

Some monitors use that philosophy to get the screen repainted quickly. This is known as *interlacing*, and, over the long haul, you won't be happy with it. When your monitor interlaces, the electron gun paints every other row: 1, 3, 5, 7, 9, and so on. Then the gun moves back up to the top and paints the alternates: 2, 4, 6, 8, etc. The result is poorer quality and perhaps an odd waver or two.

> Some manufacturers use interlacing only when monitors are displayed at the highest possible quality. For example, if your monitor is capable of displaying in SuperVGA (800 by 600) or Extended VGA (1028 by 768) and if it interlaces only in Extended mode, you may be perfectly happy with SuperVGA mode, which doesn't use interlacing.

The Rainbow Connection

Color or monochrome? Paper white or green phosphor? The choice of screen color, for many people, is the biggest consideration of monitor choice. Color monitors are prettier to look at, but many people prefer monochrome (that's single color) monitors for text work.

When color monitors first appeared, they were capable of displaying only red, green, and blue. Today, an almost unlimited number of colors are available—reaching upward of 16 million—if you have the right graphics card and monitor combination.

But not all cards or monitors can display that many colors. If you decide you want color, you can choose from several different standards. And, as you might expect, the lower the number of colors, the lower the price tag. Here's what's available:

Standard	Called	Number of Colors
4-bit color	16-color mode	16
8-bit color	Pseudo color	256

Standard	Called	Number of Colors
16-bit color	High color	32,000
24-bit color	True color	16+ million

Again, you may not need top of the line for the type of work you'll be doing (most of us don't).

They're Out To Get Us

What can happen to a monitor? For the most part, monitors seem to be pretty sturdy beasts, caving in to disrepair only after periods of extreme abuse or neglect.

Occasionally, you may hear a horror story about how somebody's monitor "fried" or get the refrain of the out-of-warranty bargain monitor that suddenly blew a tube no one sells anymore. These war stories are the price you pay for joining the ranks of computerists (something you never wanted to do anyway, right?).

Generally, if you keep these things in mind, you and your monitor should enjoy a happy life together for years to come:

- Keep all liquids away from the monitor.

- Make sure that the unit has adequate ventilation.

- Don't let your pets sleep on top—monitors are allergic to pet hair (see fig. 12.5).

Figure 12.5
The warmth and hum of the monitor make it a pleasant nest.

- Turn the monitor off or use a screen saver program when you're not using your computer (better for the environment, too).

A screen saver program is a program that turns off the display of your monitor when you haven't used your computer for a certain number of minutes (or seconds). The display is instantly returned as soon as you push any key or move the mouse. These programs offer two benefits: they keep an image from getting burned forever on your monitor, and they lessen the amount of energy being used by your computer.

- Every so often, check to make sure that the cable and power cord is tight.

- Have the system unit serviced on a regular basis to make sure that the graphics card is plugged in securely and has not accumulated any internal computer gunk.

- Make sure that you fill out and turn in the warranty card that comes with your monitor. That way, if anything does happen, you can contact the manufacturer.

Demon-stration

Pushing the Buttons

Are you on friendly terms with your monitor? Have you experimented with the little controls there on the front or side of the display? Just because someone else set the thing up doesn't mean you can't try your own settings. Go ahead. Be daring.

1. First, look for the brightness control. (It may say something like "Brite," or it may be a picture, like a sun.)

2. Turn the knob and notice which way makes it lighter. Now turn it the other way. How dark does it get? Does the background change, or do the characters darken?

3. Set the brightness to the most comfortable level for your eyes.

4. Check the contrast knob. Play around to find the best setting.

5. Find the picture placement controls, if your monitor has them. (Some monitors allow you to set where the picture is displayed horizontally on the screen, vertically, and centered.) You may not have noticed that there is actually a margin area around the screen picture on your monitor (see fig. 12.6).

Figure 12.6
*Controlling the
picture placement.*

Some monitors
allow you to
position the display
area

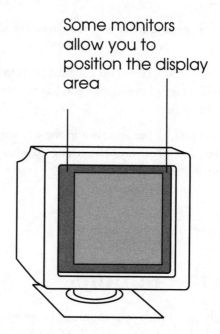

Summary

The display of your monitor is an important consideration, weighing heavily
on how much (or how little) you enjoy working with your machine. The
screen resolution, the refresh rate, the interleave factor, and the color
capability of your monitor all contribute to the overall quality of the screen
display.

Exorcises

1. What does your own comfort have to do with monitors?

2. What is the other part of the display system that translates information so that the monitor can display it?

3. Where does the graphics card go?

4. Explain refresh rate.

5. Name three things you can do to make sure that your monitor has a long life.

13th Encounter

Printer Basics 101

Goal

To introduce you to basic printer types and to explain how they do what they do.

What You Will Need

Your basic system set up and turned on; a printer, hooked up and ready to print.

Terms of Enfearment

dot-matrix printer	laser printer
PostScript	AppleTalk
thermal printer	inkjet printer
toner	printer ribbon
PCL printer	tractor feed

Briefing

Depending on the type of work you do, a printer may be an optional necessity. If you are responsible for printing reports, you'll need a printer. If you update a weekly spreadsheet and then give it to a support person to print, a printer may be an unnecessary evil.

Some offices share printers, so three or four people use a centrally located printer. If this is your situation, you probably won't have your own printer to worry about. However, the biggest group of us (speaking statistically) do have our own printers connected to our own computers. And we're responsible for buying them, running them, or both.

This encounter takes a closer look at printers. What kinds are popular? How do they work? What do you need for your own applications?

The Diligent Dot-Matrix

What a workhorse—the everyday dot-matrix printer. These handy little printers cost less than every other kind of printer available and offer features ranging from bare bones to beefy.

The dot-matrix printer gets its name from the way it prints characters and graphics on the page:

1. Paper threads through the printer.

2. Data comes from the CPU through a cable.

3. Data is sent to the printer's memory.

4. The printhead pushes pins against the ribbon, imprinting characters and graphics on the page.

As the information comes through the printer cable (from the microprocessor), the printer receives the data and forms a character by firing certain pins in a mechanism called the print head. Which pins are used depends on which character is being formed (for example, the letter A would use different pins than the letter L).

The print head then pushes the pins through a printer ribbon, leaving the imprint of the character on the page. The character looks like a pattern of dots, which it is. No matter how you look at it, a dot-matrix printer produces dots (see fig. 3.1).

> Some high-end, dot-matrix printers offer smoothing features that blend the dots together and make the characters look cleaner. Other fancy dot-matrix printer features include color capability and extremely fast print times.

Today's dot-matrix printers also support a number of fonts (*Jargon alert:* A *font* is text in a certain typeface, style, and size). Early dot-matrix printers could print only two or three kinds of type; today's printers support hundreds of fonts and print them fast, too.

The speed of the dot-matrix printer makes it a good rough draft printer. Many people use dot-matrix printers for internal documents—memos, reports, in-house training materials—because you can print them quickly and then pass them around. For finished, professional-looking documents, users often choose laser printers (explained in the next section). Nevertheless, the dot-matrix provides a quick print for editing and saves money and time in the process.

`This is an example of dot-matrix output.`

Figure 13.1
Sample dot-matrix output.

The only real downside to the dot-matrix is that one inescapable fact: everything printed on the dot-matrix printer is a pattern of dots. No matter what you do, the quality produced on that printer will be less than other standard high-end printers. Other little annoyances of the dot-matrix include that loud printing (get the earplugs) and a syndrome that will appear in your graphics known as the *jaggies*.

> Does your hand shake? Are you seeing dots before your eyes? You may be suffering from terminal jaggies—those printer-induced dots that appear everywhere on your printed copy. The only solution? A laser printer.

If what you want is a reliable, fast, economical workhorse, you'll love any good dot-matrix printer you choose. If you need something with the smoothest text and sophisticated graphics, you're looking for a different kind of printer.

The Low-Down on Lasers

Leave it to laser technology to shake things up. Before laser printers were born, we had no recourse—except Dr. Quick Print—for our professional printing needs. Sure, we could print out the 1-2-3 spreadsheet. Yes, we could do a mail-merge letter in WordStar. But have it look professional? Forget it.

Suddenly, almost overnight, everything changed. A printer was introduced that let us print high-quality text—text as good as a professional publisher would print. The laser printer gave us finely formed text and a few fonts (and we mean *few*) that were available on cartridges. Still, the quality was better than anything that had come from our desks before (see fig. 13.2).

Figure 13.2
Sample laser print.

This is an example of Laser output.

Laser printers hit the market hot and heavy and soon divided into two groups: PCL and Postscript printers. Each of these names has to do with the page description language the printer uses.

> *Jargon alert:* A page description language is the set of print instructions that explains to the printer the way the text and graphics should be printed on the page.

PCL stands for printer control language and is used primarily by the Hewlett-Packard family of computers. The earliest PCL printer was the LaserJet, which itself began a family of descendents. The first Postscript printers appeared quite a bit later, but these printers gave users the choice of scaleable fonts instead of font cartridges and up to 36 built-in fonts.

The PostScript language was different from PCL in that all the instructions in the language were based on mathematical calculations. This means that fonts can easily be placed in proportion at any size, allowing the simple resizing of fonts and graphics. This "scalable font" capability and easy manipulation of terrific graphics remains the strongest sales point of Postscript printers.

The laser printer works by receiving the information from the microprocessor through the print cable. The information then goes to the image processor, which translates the data into PCL or Postscript language. The printer then fires up the laser, which strikes a rotating mirror and is reflected into the toner cartridge where it strikes the drum, which is coated with a light-sensitive substance (see fig. 13.3). The drum rolls past a cartridge full of toner (ever heard of a toner cartridge?), and it picks up the toner on its magnetically charged surface. Then the toner is transferred to the paper, and the paper rolls out of the printer. Amazing. All done at about eight pages per minute.

Remember resolutions? We discussed them in the 12th Encounter, but we were talking about screen resolution. Print resolution is just as important—perhaps more so. The resolution of your printed characters is the number of dots used to create the image. Early laser printers were able to print at 300 dots per inch (written *dpi*). That was extremely high-quality when compared to dot-matrix output. Today's laser printers have broken that mold, offering 600, 1000, or even 1200 dpi.

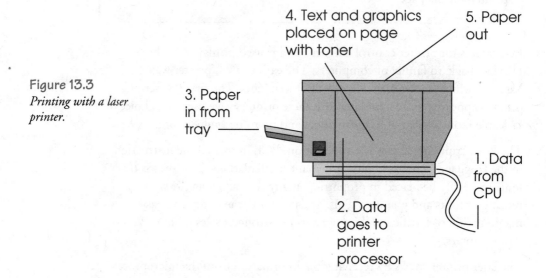

Figure 13.3
Printing with a laser printer.

3. Paper in from tray

4. Text and graphics placed on page with toner

5. Paper out

1. Data from CPU

2. Data goes to printer processor

The downside of laser printers used to be a *big* downside: cost. When they were first introduced, Postscript laser printers had price tags exceeding $4,000. PCL printers were around $2,000. Today, you can get a PCL printer for under $1,000 if you do some shopping. Similarly, PostScript printers have dropped in price, giving you everything you want for around $2,600. Today, the highest price bracket is reserved for full-color PostScript printers, the higher end of which run about $25,000.

The Miscellaneous Many

Although dot-matrix and laser printers are the most common in business settings, other types of printers are available. Two biggies—thermal transfer printers and inkjet printers—were beginning to die out but have been revitalized with new improvements in technology at an affordable cost.

Thermal transfer printers create characters and graphics by melting a wax-based ink off a ribbon and pressing it onto the page. These characters are still dot-based; they are simply placed very close together to give the illusion of single formation. The thermal printer provides good resolution, quiet printing, and cool effects for color printing.

Inkjet printers create the printed page by spraying characters and graphics in a pattern of ink dots. The printer uses ink cartridges instead of a ribbon or toner, which means that you can easily swap different colors in and out. The resolution of inkjets is high—some claim "better than laser" output. Again, the speed of the output is not as high as a dot-matrix printer could offer, but the inkjet is easier on the ears.

They're Out To Get Us

Printers can be fussy machines, but overall, the fussiness is not a "physical" one. The biggest problem new users have with their printers is getting it to print in the first place. This problem—the hang-up—is usually with the software, not the hardware.

There are so many different kinds of printers available today that program developers have to create different instructions for different printers. These instruction sets are called printer drivers. Before a program can work with your particular printer, it must have a printer driver to tell the software and the hardware how to work with each other. Without the driver, your printer may not print. Or, at least, it may not print the way you expect it to.

How do you solve this? If you haven't purchased your printer yet, look for one with a well-known name. Don't buy a printer from a bargain basement dealer who won't be around tomorrow when no one can get your printer to print. Epson, Toshiba, Panasonic—you'll recognize the names. Ask around. Find out who's been here for a while and who's most likely to stick around.

Laser printers are easier—companies like NEC, QMS, Apple, and Hewlett-Packard monopolize the laser printer market. There are, however, some smaller companies that buy the engine from other printers and put it in their own packaging. Best advice? Ask around before you buy.

Demon-strations

Preparation P

We'll all have different programs to use, and those different programs will have different print routines. In general, you'll find a Print command in the File menu, whether you're using the Mac or a PC, DOS or Windows. Before you can print anything, however, you need to have everything set up and ready.

1. Place your printer so that the paper can move freely through the printer. (This applies to dot-matrix printers only.)

2. Thread the paper through (or put it in the paper tray, for laser printers). If you're using a dot-matrix with a tractor feed and don't know how to insert the paper, see the next demon-stration.

3. Make sure that the printer cable is connected securely to the printer port in the back of the computer. (It's probably connected to LPT1.) Tighten the thumbscrews, if necessary.

4. Make sure that the power cord is plugged in.

5. Flip the power switch to On. The printer should power-up. (If not, check all your connections.)

6. Press the Print Screen key on your keyboard to get a quick printout of whatever's displayed on your monitor. The information should go to the printer immediately.

Some printers have a special Print Test button you can press to do a sample printout of all characters, numbers, and symbols. This can help you narrow down the problem when things aren't working properly and you're not sure whether it's the computer or the printer that's messing up.

Feeding the Printer

Well, you'll never get anything printed if you don't know how to get the paper in there. Don't be embarrassed—many a new and experienced user has paled in the face of an unfamiliar dot-matrix printer.

Most dot-matrix printers today have what's called a tractor-feed mechanism that pulls the paper through and keeps it straight during printing. What a great invention. You used to have to stand beside your printer during the entire print job to make sure that the paper didn't slip to the right or left. And just when you turned your back—gnash, gnarl, crunch—that beast would crumple the pages and eat the printout.

To feed the paper through the printer, follow these steps:

1. Place the paper box behind the printer.

2. Look for the tractor-feed mechanism. (On some dot-matrix printers, this is inside the unit; on others, the paper-feed extends above the printer in the rear.)

3. If necessary, lift the printer cover to get to the tractor feed.

4. Open the tractor feed. The little teeth will be exposed (see fig. 13.4).

Figure 13.4
Opening the printer's mouth.

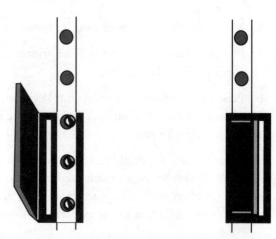

5. Thread the paper through and lay it over the teeth so that they show through the little holes along the edges of the paper.

6. Close the tractor-feed mechanism.

7. Advance the paper by turning the knob on the side of the printer or by pressing the paper advance button (if your printer has one).

8. Align the paper so that the perforation is just above the print head. Now press the on-line button, and you're ready to roll.

Summary

Printing may or may not be a regular part of your computing diet. Different kinds of printers are used today, giving us different kinds of output. Dot-matrix printers are fast and cost-effective, but loud. Laser printers give better quality and relatively quick output, but they are more expensive than dot-matrix printers. Thermal transfer and inkjet printers are two alternative printer types that have been increasing in popularity.

Exorcises

1. How does the dot-matrix printer print?

2. What are the good qualities of the dot-matrix?

3. What are jaggies?

4. How does a laser printer work?

5. What kinds of laser printers are available?

6. True or false: Thermal transfer printers form characters by spraying ink in a pattern of dots.

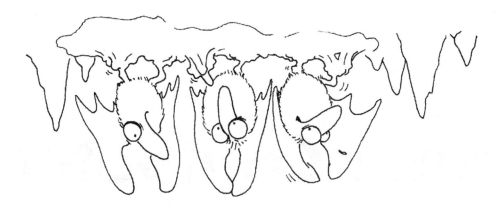

Other Computer Tools: Modems, Scanners, and Faxes

Goal

To take a look at a few other computer items you may come in contact with.

What You Will Need

Some reason to learn about modems, scanners, and faxes (!).

Terms of Enfearment

modem	modulator demodulator
baud rate	flatbed scanner
hand-held scanner	fax
color scanner	OCR software

Briefing

You've made it through all the serious hardware components. Now for the extras. Your job may involve you calling up and making airline reservations with a national information service. And that means modem. Maybe you're putting together a catalog that includes photos of merchandise. A scanner would certainly help. Or perhaps you work in an office that often sends and receives faxes right from the PC. Better find out about faxes, right?

I Can't Hear You: Modems

You're not alone—many people fear their modems. So many things in computing are done alone. If you mess up, who will know? Nothing lost.

But if you link up with a communications service and then mess up, how do you know there aren't millions of people looking on?

Everything worthwhile is a gamble.

A modem is an electronic device that allows you to use the phone lines to send and receive data to and from other computers. You can connect to a computer in another office, another city, or another country. You can link up with a private user working in a corner of her basement or a huge multimillion dollar corporation with no single person running the show.

The word *modem* is short for modulator/demodulator, which describes the process the modem goes through in changing the data into sendable and receivable form. First, the modem changes the data into audio signals by using a process called *modulation*. Then, the data signals are sent through the phone lines to the other (receiving) end, where the data is turned back into electronic data (*demodulation*).

Two kinds of modems are available: external and internal. An *external* modem sits outside the system unit of your computer; the *internal* unit fits inside and plugs into the motherboard. A phone jack is part of the modem board and extends from the back of the system unit. Rather than plugging the phone line into the wall, you plug the phone line directly into your computer (see fig. 14.1).

With a bus mouse, the phone line plugs right into the back of the system unit.

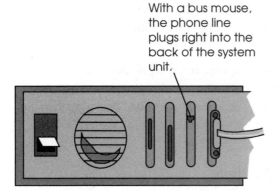

Figure 14.1
The phone line hooks directly into your computer.

Reach Out and Type Someone

What can you do with a modem? Run programs you haven't got; talk to people that aren't there; deliver a message, report, or proposal electronically when you can't be there in person. Here are a few of the ways people use modems:

- **To transfer files back and forth.** You can send a report to the home office in Boston when you're visiting Wichita by sending it through the phone lines.

- **To leave messages in an electronic mailbox.** Electronic mail, called E-mail, is one of the newest computer rages. E-mail systems may be set up within your office or on an information service that reaches the entire world. You can leave simple memos for other people and check the messages left for you.

■ **To talk to other users.** A great many computer users communicate with other users by modem. Most communities have local bulletin boards that users can call up and access, retrieving files or information about current events.

■ **To access information services.** Huge commercial databases, like CompuServe or GEnie, exist so that the millions of modem users all over the world can reach a variety of on-line resources. Want to make airline reservations? Get a stock quote? Find out the weather in Tahiti? Get the latest popular shareware game? Information services have all that—and much more.

The modem and the program you use with it (called *communications software*) make the capabilities of your computer almost unlimited. Do you have the latest stock information in your computer? No? With a modem and communications software, you can bring that information to your screen.

If You Can't Beat 'Em, Modem

So what do you do if you decide to take a shot at this connectivity craze? First, add a modem. (Talk to your local retailer about the type of modem— internal or external—that will work best for your system.)

Modems come in different speeds. The first modems pumped information through the phone lines at a molasses-like speed of 300 bps (that's bits per second). Today's transmission times are 9600 bps or even higher. As a general rule, get the fastest modem you can afford.

Next, you'll need communications software. Sometimes, manufacturers offer the software along with the modem you purchase. In some cases, you may be on your own for the software. A few good communications programs are ProComm Plus, CrossTalk, and SmartCom III.

If you want to join one of the many information services, you'll wind up paying a subscription price. Some services charge by the month; others charge by the minute. A typical fee might be $29 a month or .12 a minute before 6 p.m. and .25 a minute after 6 p.m. (And if you're investing in a modem, you should at least take a test drive through one of these information services. Amazing.)

A Trip to the Scanning Bed

Ahhh. You've been looking forward to this all week. The sound of the ocean waves pulls you just to the edge of sleep while the warmth of the tropical sun bakes all the tension from your muscles. . .

Suddenly, the sun goes out. Static crackles on a loud speaker. "Excuse me, but—time's up."

You emerge from the bed, feeling dazed and, you hope, slightly bronzed. If that strange synthetic sunlight had been doing something more than deepening your tan, if it had instead been bouncing light rays off of you in an attempt to create an electronic picture, you could say you were being scanned.

A scanner is an item you may want to add to your computer so that you can use photographs, hand-drawn art, and even pages of text in your computer files. The scanner sends out a beam of light that bounces back in different wavelengths, allowing the scanner (or, rather, the program that comes with the scanner) to "read" what's on the page. The software communicates that information to the computer, and you save the scanned image as a computer file.

Scanners, Scanners Everywhere

How many different scanners are out there? Lots. How many different types of scanners are available? Just a few:

■ **Hand-held scanners.** These represent the small end of the scale. A hand-held scanner is a device about twice the size of the mouse and that covers a little less that half a page vertically (see fig. 14.2). These are great for small items, like logos, but not so great for large images or text. Your hand wobbles too much when you're trying to scan larger items.

Figure 14.2
*The hand-held
scanner.*

New hand-held color scanners are now available, although until recently all the little fellows were gray-scale only. One popular color hand-scanner is from Logitech.

- **Half-page scanners.** This is really just an oversized hand scanner. Half-page scanners can scan—you guessed it—about half a page at a time. They are still considered hand-held and still wobble when you do.

- **Flat-bed scanners.** These larger cousins are for the Serious About Scanning. These devices are smaller than copiers but the process is similar; open the top, place the item on the glass, close the top, scan. These are the best for serious scanning because the image doesn't move—rather, it stays flat in the scanner. What's that mean? No wobbles. Flat-bed scanners are available in two varieties—gray-scale and color. Gray-scale scanners are less expensive than their color counterparts, but both are a significantly larger investment than hand-held or half-page scanners.

Scanned If You Do, and Scanned If You Don't

Scanning photos and art is different from scanning text. When you scan artwork, the art is saved in a file, and you can clean it up using your favorite paint or draw program. Text, however, is a different matter. With text, you want to be able to fix misspellings, change fonts (maybe), and reformat paragraphs if necessary. To be able to do this, you must have a different kind of program, known as OCR (optical character recognition) software. If you plan to scan text, be sure to talk to your computer dealer about the necessary software before you begin.

How much will you pay for the ability to turn things like photographs, mug shots, drawings, and research papers into computer files? The price ranges, depending on the features you want, from $129 for a hand-scanner to upwards of $10,000 for great-quality color scanners. Scanners usually come with their own scanning software, although you'll have to buy OCR software separately, and you may want to invest in a program that helps you clean up any rough edges on the images you scan.

Just the Fax, Man

What's all this fuss about faxes? It seems that just yesterday, tomorrow was soon enough.

"When can you get that to me?"

"I'll send it out tonight, and you'll get it tomorrow."

That answer was acceptable, until faxes. Those days are gone. Now the only possible answer is "I'll fax it to you right away."

Instant gratification. Ask and receive in the same instant. What's next? Transferring files before we create them?

Fax or Fiction?

All grumbling aside, faxes offer us an immediacy in our work that some of us desperately need. No longer does a designer have to await an approved page design; now he can receive the marked up pages the moment after they are approved. Lawyers can send signed documents to clients instantly; sales can be made, situations resolved, and offers accepted from all ends of the earth in literally seconds.

Two types of faxes are the rage: stand-alone faxes and fax boards for the computer. Each type has its advantages. The stand-alone fax has all sorts of special features, like special no-dial buttons for numbers you phone often or multiple function as a phone or fax (or even copier). The fax board, however, that you plug into one of the slots on your computer's motherboard, gives you the option of saving the received file as computer data so that you can use it in other applications.

Fax Shelters and Other Investments

So how much will this cost you? A stand-alone fax will run anywhere from $500 to $1,000 or more, if you want one with all the programmable buttons, special lights, and gadgets. Some discount office supply places sell stand-alone faxes for under $400 (if you catch them in a good mood or with an overstock around tax time).

A fax board is surprisingly less draining on the pocket. The average cost for a fax board is between $250 and $400. Remember that the plug-in board will use up yet another available slice of your expansion slots, so make sure that you've got the room and want to use it before you invest in a fax board.

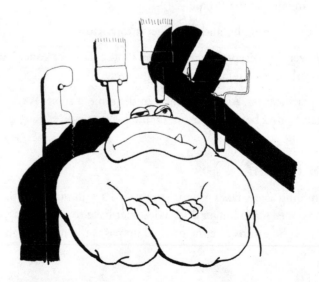

They're Out To Get Us

You won't be happy after you've spent hundreds of dollars setting up one of these speciality items if nothing works. The modem doesn't call anyone. The scanner doesn't scan. And the fax board doesn't fax.

Now what?

First things first. If the device is connected by a cable (a scanner would be, certainly, and an external modem would be as well), check to make sure that the cable connection is tight and connected to the right port.

When you're sure that you've got it plugged in the right place, check your software settings to make sure that the program thinks the cable is plugged in the right place. If you plugged the cable into COM1 when the modem board is set up to work with COM2, nothing will happen. (To find out how to check the settings of your software, consult the program's documentation.)

Okay, we're narrowing it down. If the cables are tight and plugged in the right place, you may be having a hardware problem. If possible, have a coworker test the item on a similar machine (of course, the coworker must have a computer setup similar to yours) to see whether the hardware works.

If you tried all three things and can't find the reason for the brownout, use that trusty technical support number listed in the documentation for the scanner or the modem.

If you're using a fax board and nothings happening, check the software to see whether it "sees" the board (the book will tell you how). If it doesn't, yell for tech support.

That's the best reason for not accepting a copy of software from a friend (besides the fact that it's illegal). If you use hot software, there's no technical support for you—when you're stuck, you're stuck.

Demon-stration

Take this little test, using the following rating system: 0 Not at all;
1 A little, I guess; 2 Pretty much; 3 A lot; 4 A whole lot.

About Modems:

1. How much would your business benefit from long-distance computing? _____

2. How often do you watch the Home Shopping Network? _____

3. How frequently do you want up-to-the-minute news? _____

4. How would you like easy access to the latest games (shareware and freeware)? _____

About Scanners:

1. How often do you use photographs in your work? _____

2. How frequently do you hand-draw your own art? _____

3. How much would you benefit from text scanning capabilities? _____

4. How important is it to use your company's logo on everything? _____

About Faxes:

1. How often do you use a fax? _____

2. How much time would it save you to have a fax board built into your computer? _____

3. How frequently do you work with documents that you would fax if you had one? _____

4. How often do business transactions get delayed because you don't have access to a fax? _____

Rating Your Answers

Now total your points for each section. If you had 16 or more, you need that item. If you rated 12, the item is a definite necessity you are putting off for the moment. Eight points is a middle-of-the-road call. Lower than 8 says you might be interested someday, but probably not today.

Summary

Computer systems can be more than a monitor, a system unit, and a keyboard (and mouse). Specialized tasks need more specialized computer items. A modem can link you to computers around the corner or around the world. A scanner can turn something on paper—text or art—into data in a file. A fax board can be plugged in to your computer system, giving you immediate fax advantage. Before you buy, weigh the plusses and minuses of each component and shop around to make an educated decision.

Exorcises

1. Where did the modem get its name?

2. What types of modems are available? What's the difference?

3. Name the three types of scanners. Which is best for large items?

4. What are the two types of faxes?

5. What is the primary benefit of a fax board?

What about Software?

Goal

To learn about the great and terrible things you experience with computer programs.

What You Will Need

Some interest in purchasing computer software for your system.

Terms of Enfearment

mail-order   system compatibility
application software   operating system software
shareware   freeware
installation

Briefing

You learned earlier in the book that the computer is capable of doing nothing—literally nothing—without software to run it. Software is to a computer what a CD is to a CD player. If you turn on the CD player without a CD inside, what does it do? Clunk around a little bit, but that's about all. Not a whole lot of fun, sitting around and watching the CD player spin.

Without software, the computer is a big metal paperweight, capable of many things but able to do none of them unassisted. The software tells the computer what to do, how to do it, and when to quit. (Someone more sexist than I might make a similar comparison between women and their husbands!)

So, anyway, you get the idea that software is an integral part of your computer system. There are several different kinds of software, but for purposes of discussion, we'll lump them into two main groups: application software and operating system software.

Application software tells the computer how to do a specific task (or tasks), like processing words, organizing a database, or drawing images. *Operating system software* tells the computer how to perform functions that are important for the overall processing of the machine and turns the commands you enter into information your computer can understand and use.

This encounter focuses on application software, the kind you'll purchase in a computer store (or mail-order or somewhere). The 17th Encounter explains more about operating system software.

The Hard Sell on Software

Everybody wants to sell you something (see fig. 15.1). The ads scream at you every time you open a computer magazine "New! Improved! Low upgrade cost!"

Includes Windows 3.1!
Plus the following:
* SideKick
* DOS 5.0
* Anti-virus program
* Procomm Plus
* Day Planner

FASTER!

Figure 15.1
Computer ad enthusiasm.

What They Tell You

Everyone has the best software for everything. You'll see the same PR phrases used over and over again: user friendly, easy to use, intuitive interface, programmable, etc. What do these things mean? The developers are casting their hooks.

Can we believe what the ads say? How do we know we're not investing $300 in something that is just a lot of hype?

In order to buy what you want to buy (and be reasonably secure that you're getting what you pay for), keep these things in mind as you think about making a software purchase:

■ Have you thought carefully about the kind of tasks you need to perform on the computer? (What are they?)

■ Is there a possibility that those needs could change or expand in the near future? (If so, what other features might you need?)

■ Do you have a budget to stay within?

■ Do you need to be compatible with other computers and/or software programs?

■ Have you tried the software you're considering? (Or, at least, call and ask whether the manufacturer has a demo disk so you can see the main features of the program.)

■ Have you checked the system requirements to make sure that the software will run on your computer?

What It's Like in the Trenches

After you write that check (or give that credit card number), the software is yours. You take it home and unbox it. You find manuals—perhaps two or three—along with miscellaneous annoying pieces of paper. Read those critters carefully: one is probably your software registration card; one is a card listing the technical support number and showing the program's serial number (you'll need that); and the rest is probably more advertising about the company's *other* products.

You may not want to, but you should read as much of that information as you can stand. You'll probably find a "Getting Started" booklet that tells you what to do to install the software (see fig. 15.2).

Figure 15.2

The volume of documentation may be overwhelming.

Jargon alert: Installing the software means to put the software on your computer (specifically, on the hard disk) so that you can run the program later. Many programs have their own utility that takes care of the installation for you.

After you start using the program (you learn how to start and exit a program in the next Encounter), you hope that the developers were telling the truth with all their colorful adjectives. Life in the trenches is filled with little oh-what's-the-use gremlins that confuse you at every turn. You need to indent a paragraph and can't find the command you need. You want to print in color, but the documentation doesn't explain that part. Easy to use? Intuitive? Boy, if you could get a hold of the people who wrote that ad copy, you'd set them straight . . .

Matchmaking: Hardware and Software

One of the biggest mistakes new users used to make was buying the wrong program for the wrong computer. In the early days of packaging, manufacturers weren't quite so clear about the machines needed to run their programs. It was possible to get home and realize that you'd just purchased a Mac program for your PC.

Today, the best advice is to read the box. It will tell you everything you need to know about the software (except whether it will work the way they promise). For example, the following information is included on the Macintosh version of Adobe Illustrator:

Requires: (this means that the software won't work without the following things)

- Macintosh II, LC, SE, Plus, or Classic
- Hard disk
- 2M RAM (for System 6.0.5) or 4M (for System 7.0)

Recommended: (meaning that the software will work better if you have these things)

- Macintosh with 68020 or greater microprocessor
- Color monitor
- Postscript printer and scanner
- Adobe Collector's Editions
- Adobe Streamline 2.0

This seems pretty straightforward, but some situations may baffle you. What if you want to use a program that runs in DOS but you need to import the files into Windows? For example, suppose that you are going to use Aldus PageMaker—which needs Microsoft Windows in order to run—and you're looking for a word processor to create the files you'll later layout in PageMaker. Your officemate is pushing WordStar 7.0, a program that runs in DOS, not Windows. Someone else suggests Microsoft Word, which also runs in DOS. You've got to make a decision, and you'll be the one living with it.

In this case, Microsoft Word might be a better choice than WordStar because Word's style sheets can be used directly in PageMaker (which means that you'll have less formatting to do after you open the file in the layout software). But WordStar files can be used, too (there's just more work involved).

An even better alternative might be to find a word processing program that also runs in Windows, like Microsoft Word for Windows or WordPerfect for Windows. If it's got "Windows" in the name, you can be sure that it will be compatible with Windows programs.

Yet another situation arises when you need software that's compatible with more than one type of machine. Some people use PCs but need to create files that can be used on a Mac. That's a different type of compatibility altogether.

The newer Macs have SuperDrives that are capable of working with DOS files. That doesn't mean that the software will be compatible; it means that you might be able to use the PC data in your Mac. A Macintosh product called DOS Mounter can also make the file transfer a little more comfortable.

Where Do You Get It?

Where do you buy your software? You have a few choices, depending on the type of shopper you are. Do you prefer a hands-on approach? Do you often buy mail-order? Both sides have their advantages and disadvantages.

If you purchase your software from a retail computer store or software dealer, you're paying for their overhead. Expect the software—unless you can catch it on special promotion—to be a few percentage points higher than the prices you'll see in computer magazines. You also have to deal with pushy salespeople who are more interested in making quotas than they are in your particular computing needs.

The upside of a computer retail outlet is that, in most cases, they stick around. You went to the store yesterday, so you can expect it to be there tomorrow when that software starts giving you fits. Good computer stores offer some amount of training with a substantial new software product (if you're paying more than a hundred bucks, ask for some training time if they don't offer it). Good computer stores also provide a limited amount of phone support—if you get stuck, you can call and someone "knowledgeable" will lead you back to the path of successful computering. Keep in mind, however, that the store can only help out so much; after that, you're on your own, unless you purchase an extended service contract (which they'll be glad to sell you).

Mail-order outfits have sprung up everywhere, but they seem to multiply mainly on the west coast. You'll find their ads riddling the computer magazines—big, bright obnoxious things with *CALL! CALL!* typed where prices should be. Be careful with these organizations. Some are terrific; others are terrible. Here are a few guidelines to make sure that you've got a reputable mail-order company:

- Ask them questions about the product you're ordering. How long is the price good? Does this version include font support? When is the next upgrade? Has it been a popular seller?

- Ask about their return policy. What if you get the software and don't like it? What if you make a mistake and don't have enough memory to run it? If they say *No Returns* and mean it, find a different company.

- Find out about shipping costs. Some companies will ship overnight—and free—if your order is above a certain limit. Make sure that there are no hidden costs.

Remember that these companies are competing like mad to get your business. Don't feel that you have to stick with one company just because you

called and asked them questions. Check around. Get educated. Then go
with the company that sounds the most reliable and offers the best deal.

Other types of software are extremely low-cost or even free. *Shareware*
is a type of program that is distributed based on a try-it-before-you-
buy-it philosophy. If you use and like the program (and intend to
continue using it), the developer asks that you send a small fee (usually
$25 to $50 dollars). If you don't use it, well, don't use it. *Freeware* is
another type of program that is distributed free of charge. You can
usually find shareware and freeware on bulletin boards and public
information services.

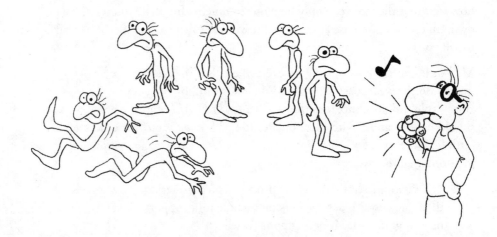

They're Out To Get Us

What can you do when you're stuck? Fuss and fume, certainly. Walk away
from your machine, count to 10, and go get a cup of coffee. (And some

Summary

Software is an integral part of your computer system. Without software, your computer is nothing more than a big, expensive paperweight. Your computer will require two kinds of software: applications software and operating system software. Buying application software can be confusing, but do some homework and make an educated decision, whether you buy from a retail outlet or a mail-order business.

Exorcises

1. What's the difference between applications software and operating system software?

2. Name three questions to consider before buying software.

3. What's the first thing you should do when you get stuck using software?

4. Name the two primary ways to purchase software.

5. What's the difference between shareware and freeware?

Starting and Exiting a Program

Goal

To help you find out how to start (and exit) an application program on your PC or Macintosh.

What You Will Need

Your computer assembled, plug in, and turned on; the program you want to use installed and ready to run.

Terms of Enfearment

power up	boot
Program Manager	DOS prompt
Finder desktop	icons
root directory	directory

Briefing

Now that you know the importance of using software, you need to know what to do with it. It would be impossible to teach the ins and outs of all the different software programs, but we can show you a few of the basics. This encounter explains how to start and exit two kinds of PC programs—one that runs in DOS and one that runs in Windows—and one Macintosh program.

Keep in mind, however, that this encounter assumes that the software has already been installed for you and is now ready to run on the hard disk. If the program you want to work with has not been installed, stop now and enlist someone to install it for you. (Or, if you have to do it yourself, follow the documentation instructions carefully.)

DOS: Launching and Landing

In this section, you'll find your way through DOS to start the Microsoft Word program. If you don't have Word, don't worry—the process for any DOS program will be similar.

> You may not see the DOS prompt when you power up if someone else has put a custom menuing system on the computer for you. If you turn on your computer and see a menu instead of the DOS prompt, skip this encounter and go on to the 17th Encounter. (Although, if it's not obvious, you might want to ask the person who set up the menu how you get into the program you want.)

Beginning with DOS

You've heard a lot of talk about an unfriendly DOS prompt. Now's your chance to meet it (see fig. 16.1).

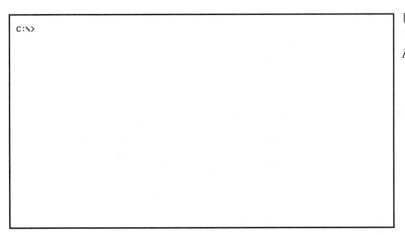

Figure 16.1
The unfriendly DOS prompt.

All DOS programs must begin at this point. The `C:\>` shown in the figure means that the root directory of the hard disk is the current location.

> *Jargon alert:* A *directory* is a section of the hard disk you set up to store similar files. The *root directory* is the main section from which all other directories split. (More about this in "Arranging Your Programs and Files," 18th Encounter.)

First, you need to move to the directory (or segment of the hard disk) where your Word files are stored. To do this, you type

    CD WORD

and press Enter. The CD stands for Change Directory, and WORD tells DOS to go to the directory named WORD.

Starting Word

It may not be obvious, but you are now "in" the Word directory. This means that the computer is ready to look in that directory for the file needed to start the Word program. To start Word, type the following command and press Enter:

WORD

After a moment, the Word opening screen appears. Then it disappears, and a blank document is there, ready to be used (see fig. 16.2).

Figure 16.2

The blank screen in Microsoft Word.

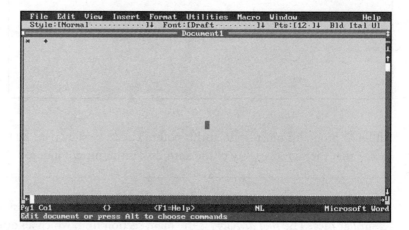

Exiting Word

After you've typed your award-winning prose, you can exit the file easily. Oops—hold on there—don't leave that file without saving! You'll find the Save command in the File menu, just a few commands above the Exit Word option, as shown in figure 16.3.

After you save (just select the command and enter a file name), open the File menu again and choose Exit Word. If you forget to save, Word will tell you that the file has changed since you last used it and ask you whether you want to save the file. If you've already saved the file, you are dumped (rather roughly) back to DOS.

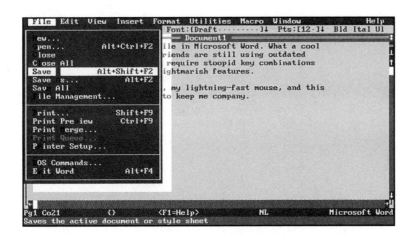

Figure 16.3
Finding the Save command and exiting a file.

Opening and Closing a Windows Program

It sounds a bit confusing, but you start Microsoft Windows from DOS, too. Yes, I know—you thought Windows was Windows and DOS was DOS. One of the benefits of using Windows is that you only have to start with DOS once (when you turn on the computer) and then you can remain blissfully in the user-friendly Windows for the rest of the day (if you use all Windows-compatible software).

Beginning with Windows

To start Windows, you begin at the DOS prompt:

```
C:\>
```

Then type *WIN* and press Enter. After a moment, the Windows Program Manager appears (see fig. 16.4). The Program Manager is—well—a manager for your programs. In this window, you'll find small pictures—called *icons*—for the groups of applications. For example, when you double-click the Accessories icon, a window opens that contains several different application programs (see fig. 16.5).

Figure 16.4
*The Windows
Program Manager.*

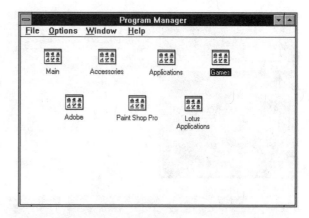

Figure 16.5
*Opening a group
window.*

Starting Paintbrush

To start a program—in this case, Windows Paintbrush—you have two
options:

■ You can click on the Paintbrush icon and then open the File menu and
choose Open.

■ You can double-click the Paintbrush icon.

Either way, Windows starts the Paintbrush program (see fig. 16.6).

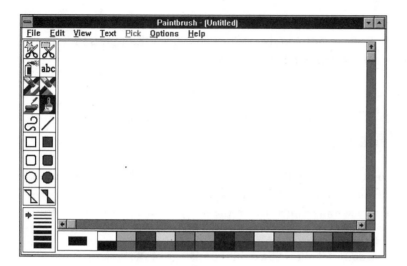

Figure 16.6
Windows Paint-brush.

Exiting Paintbrush

After you've created your masterpiece, remember to save the file. Again the Save command is in the File menu. When you want to exit the program, you can use one of two methods:

■ Open the File menu and choose the Exit command (see fig. 16.7).

■ Move the pointer to the small box in the upper left corner of the window (called the control-menu box) and double-click.

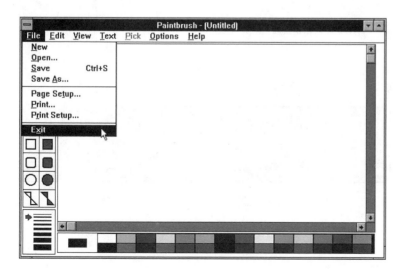

Figure 16.7
Exiting Paintbrush.

Windows will warn you that you're about to leave the program and ask whether you really want to do that. When you click OK or press Enter, you are returned to that unfriendly DOS prompt.

MacStarting and MacExiting MacPrograms

Mac programs, as you might expect, are different from DOS and Windows programs. If you're coming to the Mac after having some Windows experience, you'll notice some similarities in the way you interact with the software involved.

The entire Macintosh look is based on the analogy of the desktop (not unlike Windows). From the moment you turn on the Mac, that desktop greets you, complete with its icons, folders, and menu bar (see fig. 16.8).

Figure 16.8
The Macintosh desktop.

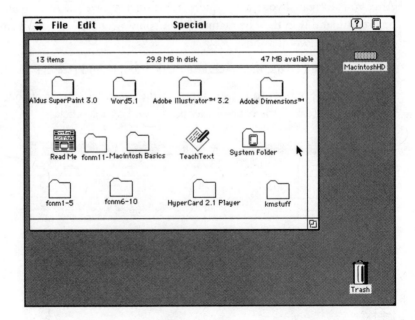

Starting SuperPaint

To start a program on the Macintosh, simply position the mouse pointer on
the program icon you want to choose and double-click the mouse button.
For this example, we're selecting Aldus SuperPaint.

You can also start programs on the Mac by clicking the icon once
(highlighting it) and then opening the File menu and choosing Open.

The folder opens, revealing the Aldus SuperPaint 3.0 window (see fig. 16.9).
In the top left corner of the window, you see the program icon. A document
explaining the product history and four other folders are also present. To
start the program, either double-click the program icon or click the icon
once, open the File menu, and choose Open. After a moment, the Super-
Paint screen appears.

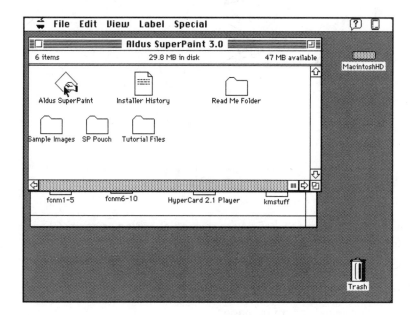

Figure 16.9
*Starting Aldus
SuperPaint.*

Exiting SuperPaint

When you're ready to exit the program, open the File menu and choose Quit. If you prefer, you can press the quick key Command-Q. You are then returned to the Macintosh desktop.

They're Out To Get Us

What could possibly happen when you're starting or exiting programs? Several things:

Nothing. You start the program, and the computer just sits there, staring at you. Or perhaps you get an unfriendly message:

```
Bad command or file name
```

First, don't panic. It may be that you forgot to change to the directory in which the program files are stored. (Remember that before you entered WORD to start Microsoft Word you used the CD command to change to the WORD subdirectory?) Make sure that you're in the right subdirectory before you enter the command to start the program.

On the Mac, you may see a pop-up window that tells you that you don't have enough memory to run a certain application. (This can happen in Windows, too.) If you've got other programs open, close those programs and then restart the program you want to use.

If you enter the command to start the program and your display goes away (and doesn't come back), the program may not work with the display card you use. If this happens, call technical support for help.

Demon-strations

Starting a DOS Program

1. If you're using DOS, use the CD command to change to the directory storing the program files.

2. Type the command to start the program and press Enter.

Starting a Windows Program

1. At the DOS prompt, type *WIN* and press Enter.

2. When the Program Manager appears, double-click on the group window icon you want to open.

3. Double-click on the icon of the program you want to start.

Starting a Macintosh Program

1. From the Mac desktop, double-click on the application icon.

2. When you see the program icon, double-click it.

Summary

The process for starting programs—whether you're using a PC equipped with DOS or Windows or the Macintosh—is a simple one that basically stays the same from program to program. Exiting is even easier. Remember, however, to save your work before you exit an application program.

Exorcises

1. What does `C:\` mean?

2. What is a directory?

3. What is the command for changing to the directory in which the program files are stored?

4. What is the name of the main window in Microsoft Windows?

5. The Macintosh uses what analogy for its display?

17th Encounter

What Is an Operating System?

Goal

To explore the fact and fiction of operating systems and to determine how rarely you'll have to come in contact with one.

What You Will Need

Your computer up and running; the operating system ready to beep at you.

Terms of Enfearment

user interface	DOS Shell
UNIX	multitasking
multiuser	System 7
OS/2	Finder

Briefing

Let's break down the rest of the mystery. You learned about application software—the programs that allow you to perform the specific tasks you'll have to accomplish with your computer. Now it's time to find out about the mysterious interpreter that changes your commands into a language your computer understands. The operating system of your computer performs a number of functions, most of them behind the scenes.

Smooth Operator

What does the operating system do? Three basic things:

- Interacts with application programs
- Performs file management functions
- Performs disk management functions

When the operating system serves as the link between you and your applications software, it provides you with a launch pad for programs you start and exit. In the last encounter, you started Microsoft Word from DOS, and you returned to DOS when you exited the program. Similarly, you started Aldus SuperPaint from the Mac's desktop and returned to the desktop when you finished with the program. This start-and-end point is the interaction function of the operating system.

Additionally, the operating system gives you a way to work with the files you create in application programs. For example, after you create a bunch of files in Word, you need some way of working with them. You might want to copy a file or delete it: that's a function of the operating system. You might want to rename a group of files or move them to a different directory. Who's responsible? The operating system.

Another function of the operating system is your basic disk-maintenance tasks. Before you can store information on a disk, for example, you have to format that disk. You use the operating system to do the formatting.

Additionally, you can erase a disk or copy an entire disk by using operating system commands.

The Ones We Know About

You've seen the three most popular operating systems mentioned in several places in this book already: DOS (both PC DOS and MS-DOS), the Macintosh Finder, and Microsoft Windows.

Sort of.

Except that Windows isn't really an operating system, it's an environment—a program. A program that runs within another operating system—DOS.

But many people call Windows an operating system because it functions in much the same way. With Windows, you can start programs. When you exit—there you are, back in Windows. You can work with files and disks in Windows. In fact, you can do just about all your work in Windows, if you've got the programs to manage it. Just because popular opinion calls Windows an operating system (and who are we to go against popular opinion?), we'll discuss Windows as though it were an operating system in this section.

DOS

The original IBM PC came equipped with DOS, the original disk operating system. Two flavors of DOS existed: PC DOS, packaged and promoted by IBM, and MS-DOS, developed, packaged, and promoted by Microsoft.

The early versions of DOS were difficult to master: users had to remember cryptic commands and enter them at a bare DOS prompt (see fig. 17.1). As subsequent versions were released, DOS became friendlier; then, with DOS 4.0, the makers of DOS introduced the DOS Shell, an interface that allowed users to select commands from menus, escaping the earlier command-prompt necessity, although that was still an option for those who preferred it (see fig. 17.2).

Figure 17.1
The DOS prompt.

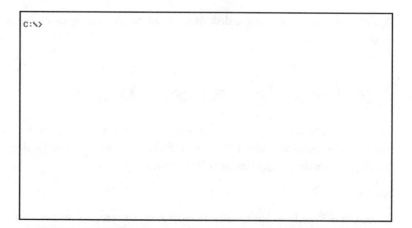

Figure 17.2
The DOS Shell.

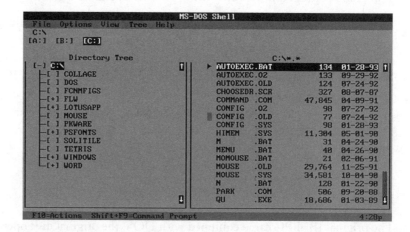

The newest version of DOS, DOS 6.0, brings some additional utilities to the operating system. Now DOS includes disk compression features, antivirus check, on-line help, easy installation, and two new commands (MOVE and DELTREE).

Finder/System 7.1

The Macintosh Finder was first introduced in 1984, the first operating system for the new Macintosh. The operating system was revolutionary then and continues to be the interface of choice for millions of happy Mac users.

The Finder is built on the analogy of the desktop. The hard disk and floppy disks are represented as icons; you double-click on them to see their contents displayed in a window (see fig. 17.3). Folders store programs and files; you double-click the folder to display its contents.

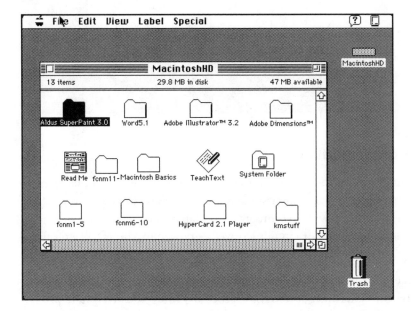

Figure 17.3
The Finder desktop.

The software responsible for the workings of the Finder is the System Software. The most current version of System Software (the one included on new Macs) is System 7.1. With the introduction of System 7.0, the Finder went through an overhaul; now users had multicolored icons, a customizable Apple menu, and a feature known as Balloon help (see fig. 17.4). Other enhancements to System 7.1 include TrueType fonts (a special font technology that lets you create fonts in any size) and QuickTime, a special feature for using video in your applications.

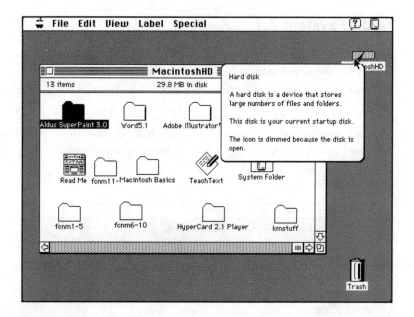

Figure 17.4
Balloon help.

Microsoft Windows

Microsoft Windows didn't burst into the market with the kind of fanfare you might expect. In fact, the first version of Windows didn't do too well. There weren't many Windows programs available; and the environment took up too much memory in our less well-endowed machines. As a result, the program was slow and cumbersome.

Subsequent versions of Windows drastically improved both the product and the response. Windows got faster, used memory more effectively, and provided a common ground for more up-and-coming applications. Developers began creating programs that would run in the environment, providing users with a consistent interface.

Windows 3.1, the latest version of Windows, includes the Program Manager, a jumping-off point for running Windows applications (see fig. 17.5). This version of Windows, which has enjoyed sweeping success, runs on 386 and 486 machines and includes multimedia support and an automatic installation procedure.

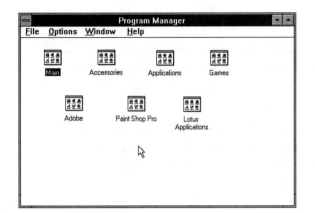

Figure 17.5
*The Program
Manager in
Windows 3.1.*

The Ones We Don't Know About

The three we just covered—DOS, Finder, and Windows—are by far the
three most common operating systems for general use. Other operating
systems are used for more specialized purposes.

OS/2

Several years ago, IBM and Microsoft began a joint venture, developing a
new operating system for the PS/2 line of IBM personal computers. This
operating system was going to set the computing world on its proverbial ear.
OS/2, which is short for Operating System 2, came into the world with little
more than a whimper.

What happened? OS/2 wasn't supported by enough applications to make
the operating system a viable alternative to DOS. The biggest sales catch to
OS/2 was the possibility of *multitasking*—the capability to perform more
than one task at the same time. Another benefit of OS/2 was the capability
to use large amounts of memory. Today, OS/2 is out there but still largely
unrecognized as a primary operating system.

UNIX

Another specialized operating system, UNIX, was designed by programmers for programmers. As such, you'll probably never come in contact with it (unless you're considering the NeXT computer, which uses UNIX as its operating system).

UNIX is often used for extremely high-end sophisticated applications, allowing multitasking and multiuser (more than one user at a time) features. UNIX also has intricate security systems, which make it a good candidate for sensitive corporate environments.

They're Out To Get Us

Generally, operating systems work the way they are supposed to—your computer is counting on it. You may run into a few strange situations now and then, however. DOS is known for its terse error messages; Windows and the Mac both take more time explaining what went wrong (or what you should check).

Some problems are simple, like conflicts in versions of software. For example, one friend recently upgraded his version of DOS. Some of the DOS commands from the old version were still on his hard disk (although he didn't know it), and when he tried to enter a few commands, he kept getting an error. With a little investigation, he was able to locate the old commands and remove them. The moral? When you upgrade to a new system, make sure that all of the old one is removed.

Some problems are hardware related, like insufficient memory. Both Windows and the Mac will give you trouble when you don't have enough RAM to run the application you're attempting. You can try rebooting the computer to remove any memory-resident programs in use, but if you still get the error, you may be looking at adding to your computer's memory.

If your computer boots mechanically but doesn't do anything software-wise, there may be something wrong with the operating system software. If you're using a DOS machine, there may be a problem with either AUTOEXEC.BAT or CONFIG.SYS, two files DOS needs in order to run properly. Turn everything off and insert a DOS boot disk in drive A. Then turn the system back on. If the system boots normally, the operating system on your hard disk is having trouble. If you still have the same problem, you'd better call for backup.

Demon-strations

Trying DOS

Let's try a few DOS commands:

1. At the DOS prompt (C:\), type *DIR* and press Enter. The files in the current directory should appear on the screen.

2. Now type *CHKDSK* and press Enter. Information about the amount of available memory appears on the screen.

3. Now type *DOSSHELL* and press Enter. The DOS Shell menu system appears on your screen.

4. Exit DOS Shell by opening the File menu and choosing Exit.

Pacing the Mac

The Macintosh is even easier to use:

1. Display the contents of the hard disk by double-clicking on the hard disk icon.

2. Open a folder by double-clicking it.

3. Open the View menu by positioning the pointer on the menu name and pressing and holding down the mouse button.

4. Choose the "by Small Icon" option. The items in the folder are displayed as small icons.

5. Return the icons to normal size by opening the View menu and choosing by Icon.

Summary

The operating system of your computer is a home base for programs, an organizer for files, and a manager for disks. Different kinds of operating systems are used on personal computers, with DOS, the Finder, and Windows (which isn't a true operating system) being the most popular.

Exorcises

1. Name the three basic functions of an operating system.

2. What operating systems are most popular?

3. Why isn't Windows a true operating system?

4. True or false: OS/2 was written for mainframe computers.

5. Name three new features of the Mac's System 7.0 operating system.

WARNING!
QUICKSAND

18th Encounter

Disk Duties

Goal

To find out how to use the operating system of your computer to perform basic disk maintenance tasks.

What You Will Need

Your computer turned on, one blank unformatted disk, and the operating system level active. (No application program running, in other words.)

Terms of Enfearment

directory list   FAT
format   dialog box
initialize   label
capacity

Briefing

The last encounter introduced you to your computer's operating system. This encounter helps you put it through its paces by performing some simple disk procedures. Some things are inescapable—if you use computers, you will be responsible for preparing disks. And after you prepare them, you need to be able to work with them. That's what this encounter is all about.

We've chosen to lump together the various procedures for each of the Big Three operating systems (or what we're *calling* operating systems: DOS, the Finder, and Windows). That means that within the DOS section, for example, you'll find sections on formatting a disk, copying a disk, and displaying disk contents. In the Mac section, you'll find the same sections, written from a Mac perspective. And in the Windows section. . .well, you get the idea.

> Before disks can store your data, you need to prepare them to record information. This process is known as *formatting* the disk.

Doing Disks with DOS

Starting at ground zero in your computer experience, there are three basic disk maintenance tasks you need to worry about:

- Formatting the disk
- Finding out what's on the disk
- Copying the disk

The one to tackle first is the one that prepares the disk to store the information: formatting.

DOS: Formatting a Disk

Formatting a disk prepares it to store the information your computer will eventually write to it. Whether you purchase 5.25- or 3.5-inch disks, low- or high-density, the disks will need to be formatted.

> You can purchase disks that have been preformatted, but experts recommend against this, claiming such disks can increase your risk of catching a computer virus.

When you use the DOS command line to format a disk, you place the disk in drive A, close the drive door (if the drive *has* a door), and then type the following command and press Enter:

```
FORMAT A:
```

If the disk is in drive B (for example, you want to format a 3.5-inch disk and the 3.5-inch drive is drive B), you use the following command instead:

```
FORMAT B:
```

> Never type *FORMAT C:* and press Enter. That tells DOS to erase everything on your hard disk!

DOS tells you to put the new disk in the drive (which you've already done) and press Enter when you're ready to format. After you press Enter, DOS begins to format the disk. Depending on the version of DOS your computer uses, DOS may display information telling you what percentage of the disk has been formatted. When the format is complete, DOS tells you the amount of disk space on the disk and asks whether you would like to format another disk.

DOS: Copying a Disk

Copying a disk in DOS is also a simple process. If you're using two disk drives (of equal size), put the disk you want to copy in drive A and the blank disk in drive B. (Get it? You want to copy A onto B.)

Now, at the DOS prompt, type the following and press Enter:

```
DISKCOPY A: B:
```

DOS makes a complete duplicate of the disk in drive A.

Jargon alert: The disk you're copying from is known as the *source* disk. The disk you're copying to is the *target* disk.

DOS: Displaying Disk Contents

Now that you know how to get data to "stick" to disks and how to copy the data on there, you need to be able to figure out what files the disk is storing. A directory list will take care of that for you. You can display a directory list—or a list of all files in the current directory—by typing the following command and pressing Enter:

```
DIR A:
```

This tells DOS to display a directory of the files on the disk in drive A. If the disk you want to explore is in drive B, of course, you would enter *DIR B:* instead.

Macintosh Maintenance

You've heard the familiar refrain before: the Mac makes things easy. Taking care of your disks on the Macintosh is not only simple, it's fun. Close to video game fun. (If you like video games.)

Mac: Formatting a Disk

You don't have to worry about accidentally trying to write data to an unformatted Mac disk—the Mac recognizes an unprepared disk the moment it's inserted in a drive. Put the disk in there, and the Mac says, "Hold on a minute. Let's fix this thing."

On a Macintosh, the term isn't *formatting*, it's *initializing*. You don't format a Mac disk, you initialize it. What's the difference? The spelling.

When the Mac determines that the disk is unformatted, it displays a message that it can't read the dang disk. You are asked whether you want to initialize it (see fig. 18.1). If you do, click the Initialize button. If you don't, click the Eject button to make the drive spit the disk out.

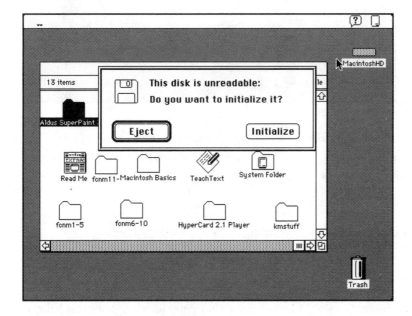

Figure 18.1
Initializing a Mac disk.

After you click Initialize, the Mac warns you that the process will erase any information previously stored on the disk (such a polite little system). If that's OK with you, click Erase (otherwise, click Cancel).

Finally, the Mac asks you to name the disk (see fig. 18.2). You can use up to 27 characters for the name, including spaces. The first character of the name must be a letter, though. If you prefer not to name the disk, you can click OK or press Return without entering a name.

Figure 18.2
*Naming a Mac
disk.*

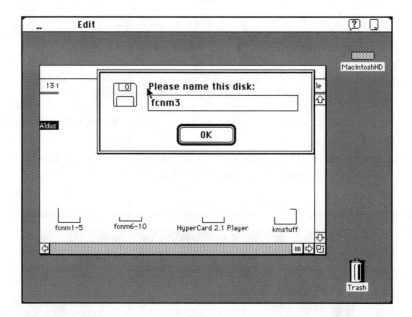

The Mac then begins formatting—oops, initializing the disk. The little watch appears, warning you to wait patiently and not pound any keys. After roughly 20 seconds, the message

        Verifying Format. . .

appears, and the computer's grunting quickens. Finally, a message

        Creating Directory. . .

is displayed, and—voila!—you're done. The disk icon (complete with the name you entered or `Untitled`, if you didn't enter anything) appears below the hard disk icon in the upper right corner of the desktop.

> You can name a Mac disk anytime, so if you missed your chance during the initialization process, don't despair. To name the Mac disk, simply click on the name Untitled. A white box surrounds the name. Now type the name you want.

Mac: Copying a Disk

Hmmm. How do you copy the contents of a disk to another disk when you've only got one disk drive on your Mac?

No big secret. First, start out with the disk you want to copy. (That's the source disk, remember?) Place it in the drive. The disk appears on the desktop, just below the hard disk icon. Now open the Special menu and choose the Eject Disk command. The disk pops out but remains on the desktop. (This is because the information on the disk is still stored in RAM.)

Now put the disk you want to copy to (the target disk) in the drive. It also appears on the desktop. Position the pointer on the icon of the first disk and drag the icon on top of the second disk (see fig. 18.3). When you release the mouse button, the Mac asks you whether you want to replace the contents of the second disk with the contents of the first. If you do, click Yes.

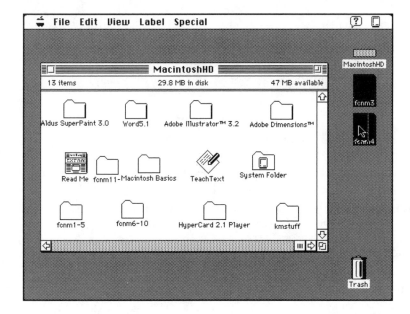

Figure 18.3
Copying a Mac disk.

Mac: Displaying Disk Contents

True to form, the technique for displaying the contents of a Mac disk is so simple it would be easy to overlook. You've got the disk on the desktop, but you don't know what's on it. Want to find out? Double-click on the disk icon. A window pops open, displaying the contents of the disk (see fig. 18.4).

Figure 18.4
Displaying the contents of a Mac disk.

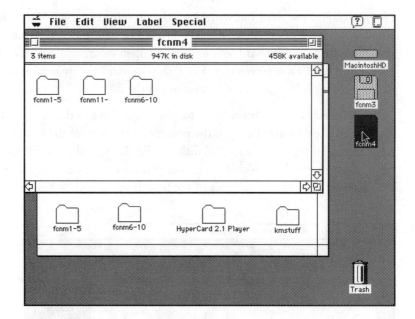

The Windows Way

Microsoft Windows uses a special utility called the File Manager to perform disk maintenance chores. You get to the File Manager by double-clicking the Main group icon and then double-clicking the File Manager icon (see fig. 18.5).

When the File Manager is displayed (notice the similarity between this and the DOS Shell?), you can select commands in the Disk menu to perform the tasks you want.

Windows: Formatting a Disk

When you want to format a disk, start by opening the Disk menu. Choose the Format Disk command. The Format Disk dialog box appears (see fig. 18.6).

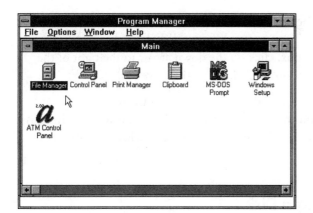

Figure 18.5
*Starting the File
Manager.*

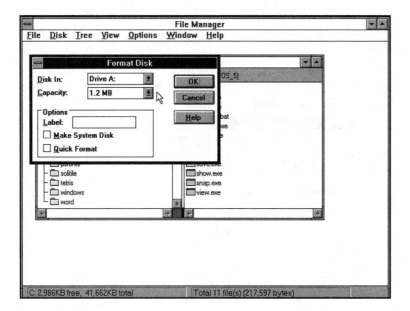

Figure 18.6
*Formatting in
Windows.*

Jargon alert: A *dialog box* is the name for a pop-up box that appears in
the center of the screen.

In the Format Disk dialog box, you first choose the disk drive holding the disk you want to format. To choose a different disk drive than the one displayed in the Disk In: box, click on the down arrow to the right of the box; then make your selection by clicking on the drive you want.

Next, choose the capacity of the disk (again, click on the down-arrow and make your choice). If you want to add a label to the disk (the same thing as a disk name), type it in the Label: box. When you're finished entering settings, click OK.

Windows: Copying a Disk

When you want to copy a disk, display the File Manager and open the Disk menu. Then choose the Copy Disk command. The dialog box shown in figure 18.7 appears.

Figure 18.7
Copying a disk in Windows.

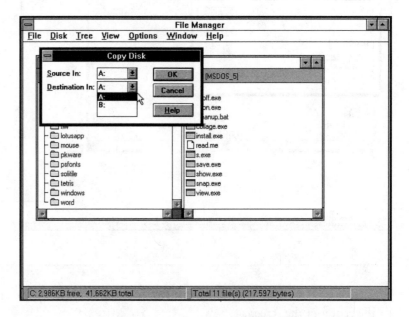

Choose the source disk and the destination (target) disk; then click OK. Windows asks you to confirm that you want the copy procedure to proceed. When you click OK, Windows completes the copy.

Windows: Displaying Disk Contents

You use the File Manager also to display the contents of disks and directories. Remember when you displayed the File Manager by double-clicking its icon in the Main group window? (The File Manager should still be displayed on the screen.)

The File Manager screen displays different kinds of information about the current directory. On the left side of the screen, you see an outline of all directories and subdirectories on the hard disk. The current directory is highlighted with a rectangle (and the file folder looks open). On the right side of the screen numerous files are listed, showing the contents of the current directory (see fig. 18.8).

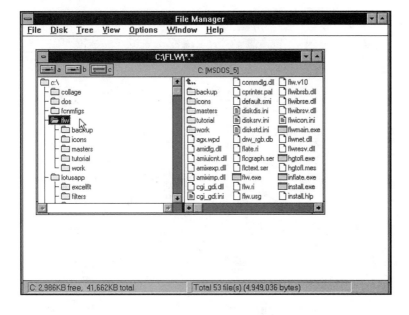

Figure 18.8

The File Manager display.

To display the contents of a disk in either drive A or drive B, simply insert the disk in the drive and click on the appropriate drive icon in the upper left corner of the screen. The File Manager then displays the files on the disk you selected (see fig. 18.9).

Figure 18.9
Displaying disk contents in Windows.

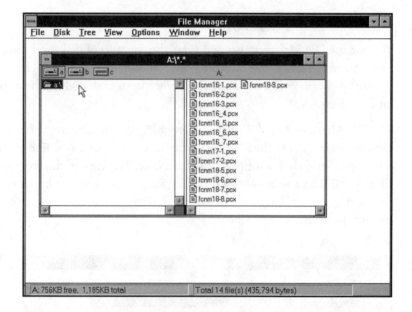

They're Out To Get Us

What can go wrong when you're working with disk maintenance tasks?

Well, you could have a bad disk. It does happen. For no reason, the blasted thing won't format. You get some kind of unfriendly error:

```
Invalid media or Track 0 bad - disk unusable
```

Or something like

```
Error reading directory
```

In both cases, you've got a bad disk. In the first case, there's probably a bad spot on the disk that's in a particularly sensitive place: track 0. The second error message occurs when DOS can't read the FAT (file allocation table) on the disk. (Remember that? It's like a table of contents DOS uses to find your files.) In either case, you can try using FORMAT again. If the FORMAT doesn't take, throw the disk away. It's hopeless.

Windows may display a variety of disk error messages, most of them pretty friendly compared to DOS. If you see something like the following, chances are that it's because the disk is write-protected (or trashed):

```
Cannot format disk
```

Check to see whether there is a write-protect tab over the notch on a 5.25-inch disk (or the switch on the 3.5-inch disk is flipped). If the disk is not write-protected and you still get the error, there is a problem with the disk. Try to reformat it by using the Format Disk command in the File Manager's Disk menu. If that doesn't work, File 13.

Demon-strations

You can never have too many formatted disks. Let's try formatting a new disk in each of the Big Three (use whatever you have available):

DOS Format

1. Get a blank, unformatted disk (5.25- or 3.5-inch)
2. Insert the disk in the appropriate drive.

3. Type *FORMAT A:* (or B:).

4. Press Enter.

5. When DOS tells you to insert the disk and press Enter, press Enter a second time.

Mac Initialize

1. Put a blank, unformatted 3.5-inch disk in the drive.

2. When the Mac asks you whether you want to initialize the disk, click the Initialize button.

3. When the Mac tells you the process will overwrite existing files, click Erase.

4. Enter a name for the disk and click OK.

Windows Format

1. From the Program Manager, double-click the Main group icon.

2. Double-click the File Manager icon in the Main window.

3. Open the Disk menu.

4. Choose the Format Disk command.

5. Select the drive holding the disk you want to format.

6. Choose the capacity for the disk.

7. Click OK.

Summary

Part of the agony your computer will put you through involves working with disks. Whether you use the 5.25- or 3.5-inch variety, you have to deal with formatting, copying, and displaying contents of disks. And that's only part of it. You also have to think about keeping track of your files. (Collective sigh.) Read on. . .

Exorcises

1. What are the three DOS commands discussed in this encounter?

2. Put the following items in the proper sequence (1 through 5):

   _____ The Mac asks whether you want to initialize the disk.

   _____ You are asked to name the disk.

   _____ The Mac tells you disk contents will be erased.

   _____ You insert the disk.

   _____ The format is completed.

3. You copy a Mac disk by _____.

   a. Opening the Special menu and choosing the Copy Disk command.

   b. Dragging the source disk icon to the target disk icon.

   c. Opening the source disk icon, dragging the contents to the hard disk, and then dragging the contents to the target disk.

4. True or false: Windows uses the File Manager to format, copy, and display the contents of disks.

5. True or false: Windows provides no command for copying entire disks.

Arranging Files and Folders

Goal

To help you learn some basic file organization techniques and to prepare for file overload.

What You Will Need

Your computer turned on, operating system active, and—if possible—a few files. (If you haven't created any yet, don't worry about it.)

Terms of Enfearment

files	root directory
subdirectories	group windows
directory tree	document files
folders	
program files	

Briefing

A file seems innocent enough when you start working with it. Little do you realize that it takes on a life of its own when it has a purpose —storing your information. Soon that one file becomes 10 files, 20 files, a hard disk full of files. Spontaneous generation? Possibly. (What are they doing in there when you're not looking?)

Soon, you have so many files that they begin getting lost. You don't remember what you named the report you wrote last month. Remember the letter to Aunt Alice? Where in the world did you save that thing?

The file lives in a place called a *directory*. The directory is a portion of a larger place (your hard drive). The directory is like a suburb of a larger city (and you know how folks in suburbia can be). You need some method of not only organizing those files into their respective neighborhoods but also of drawing a map so that you can find your way there again when you need to.

This encounter explains how you can use the Big Three operating environments (once again, DOS, the Mac, and Windows) to arrange your files and folders so that they don't drive you crazy.

> Best advice? Think about the way you want to organize your files *before* you begin and start off on the right foot. Then stick with it. As soon as you start dumping files where they don't belong ("Oh, I'll remember to clean this up later," you say confidently), it's the beginning of the end.

DOS: Simple Stuff

What kind of tasks—specifically—fall under the category of "arranging files"? First and foremost, working with directories.

A directory is a portion of your hard disk that stores files. You can put any files in any directory you choose, but hopefully you'll choose to put similar files together. For example, suppose that you're working on a quarterly report. You might lump all those files in a directory named REPORT. For the weekly spreadsheet, you might have another directory (called SPREAD, maybe). And so on.

Tripping Over the Root Directory

The Big Kahuna of your hard disk is called the *root directory*. This is the primary level from which all other directories split. Sound confusing? Take a look at a picture and see whether it helps things any (see fig. 19.1).

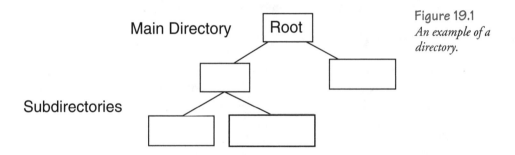

Figure 19.1
An example of a directory.

The root directory is the first level. You can store files in the root directory, although most people avoid doing that. If you plop files there, you wind up with this collage of things that doesn't make any sense. Better to put those files away in their respective directories.

> Two exceptions to the no-files-in-the-root-directory rule are AUTOEXEC.BAT and CONFIG.SYS. These two files are needed by DOS at startup; putting them in the root directory keeps your computer from getting confused.

So if you don't store *files* in the root directory, what *do* you store there?

Other directories.

Creating Directories

Before you can use directories, you have to create them. Chances are, when your machine arrived on your desk, the hard disk was already divided into several directories. You may have a directory named DOS (where the DOS files are stored) and another named WINDOWS (or WIN). Or not. Somebody initially created those directories.

When you want to create a directory for your files, you use the DOS command MD (short for make directory). You type the command, a space, and the directory name; then press Enter. For example, the following line creates a directory named FRED after you press Enter:

```
MD FRED
```

Now you've got a directory named FRED. But how do you get there?

Changing Directories

DOS always wants you to change to a directory before you do anything with the files there. For example, if you want to rename a file in FRED, you have to change to FRED before you can get to the file. Get it? Because of the verbiage used in most computer books, the phrase "change to the FRED directory" is widely accepted. But what we really mean is that you have to make FRED the current directory so that DOS knows which directory it's supposedly looking in.

To change to FRED, you use another simple DOS command: CD (for change directory). It goes like this:

```
CD FRED
```

That makes FRED the current directory.

CD can also be used to tell you what directory you're in. On many computers, the DOS prompt shows the current directory. For example, when you're in FRED, the DOS prompt shows C:\FRED>. Not all computers do this. And if yours is one of those, you'll need some way of finding out which directory you're in. Use CD to do that. Just type CD and press Enter, and DOS will display the current directory.

Erasing Directories

There may be a time when you don't need a particular directory any longer.
You're ready to say goodbye to FRED and free up some storage space on
your hard disk. To do that, you use the DOS RD (for remove directory)
command, like this:

    RD FRED

That removes FRED from the hard disk, providing that FRED is empty. If
files are stored in FRED, you'll have to delete those files before you can
delete FRED. Otherwise, you'll get an error message (see fig. 19.2).

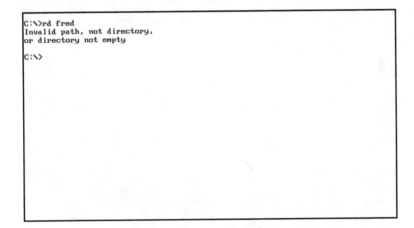

Figure 19.2
*Don't delete FRED
while he's full.*

You enter a path statement to tell DOS where to find the files (or
directory) you're working with. The path leads DOS through the
necessary subdirectories, like this:

    C:\FRED\BOOKFILES

This path tells DOS that BOOKFILES is a subdirectory of the FRED
directory, which is a subdirectory of the root directory (\). Remember
to include all subdirectory names (and the separator, \) in paths.

Macintosh: Files, Folders, and Fun

Life with the Macintosh is so much more visual than life on a PC. Here, you've got folders and desktops; there, you've got a blinking cursor and a blank screen. The Macintosh uses the analogy of the desktop to provide you with a computer environment you'll be comfortable with (see fig. 19.3).

Figure 19.3
The Macintosh desktop.

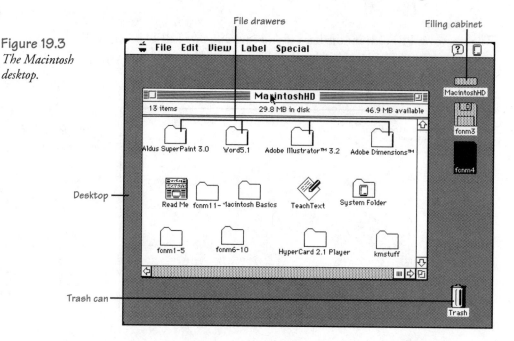

The gray area of the screen is the open desktop. In this figure, the contents of the hard drive are shown. The hard disk—or, rather, the information stored there—could be compared to the information in your traditional filing cabinet. Each item is filed away according to the drawer it belongs in. In this example, the filing cabinet has four drawers:

- SuperPaint
- Word5.1
- Illustrator
- Dimensions

Now if you opened one of those drawers by double-clicking it, you'd see the contents (see fig. 19.4). Now you're looking at the files in the Word drawer. Some of these files are *program files*—like the Microsoft Word icon—and some are *document files*. Program files start programs when you double-click them; document files open so that you can read their contents.

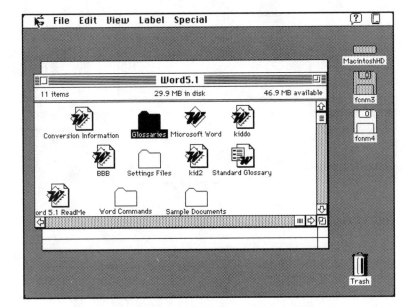

Figure 19.4
*Opening the Word
file drawer.*

Although we're making a distinction here between file drawers and file folders, to the Mac, they are all folders. You can have a folder that stores all the Word files and a folder within that folder that stores the Word program file. For example, when the desktop area is blank, double-click on the hard drive to display the four basic folders. One of those, as you saw in figure 19.3, was the Word5.1 folder. (This is level 1.)

When you double-click the Word5.1 folder, you see a variety of files and folders. (This is level 2.) Now, if you double-click on the Glossaries folder, you'll see yet another window of files. (This is level 3.) All of these are called folders, and you can create, name, select, or delete a folder on any level at any time (see fig. 19.5).

Figure 19.5
*Different folder
levels.*

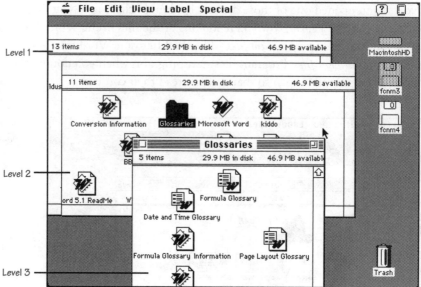

Adding a Folder

When you want to add a folder to your Mac's desktop, first move to the
level on which you want the folder to appear. For example, if you want to
create a folder to store your Word files, you might go to level 2 to create it.
How do you do this? Double-click on the Word5.1 icon. The Word5.1
window opens.

How can you tell whether a window is active? The name appears at the
top of the window, and the area in the title bar on either side of the
name is striped. When the window is not active, the title bar appears
blank beside the window name.

Now you can add the folder by opening the File menu and choosing New
Folder. (You can also press Command-N, if you prefer.) The Mac adds a
folder in the open window. It's title, `untitled folder`, is enclosed in a
white rectangle. You can rename the folder by simply typing a new name
(see fig. 19.6).

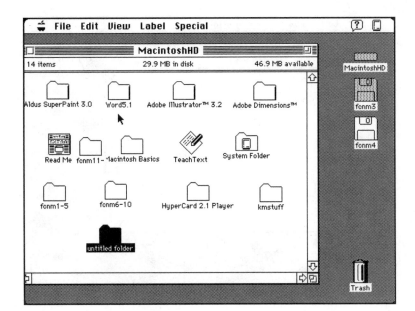

Figure 19.6
Adding a folder.

Changing to a Folder

When you want to change to the folder you just selected, all you have to do is double-click it. The folder is opened on the screen, whether you've got files already stored in there or not.

Erasing a Folder

When you're finished with a folder, dump it in the trash. Literally. Just grab the thing with the mouse and drag it down to the trash can in the lower right corner of the screen. A little outline of the folder follows the mouse; when the trash can turns black, you've got the file in the right place. Release the mouse button, and the file moves to the trash. The trash can gets fat when it needs to be emptied (see fig. 19.7).

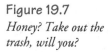
Figure 19.7
*Honey? Take out the
trash, will you?*

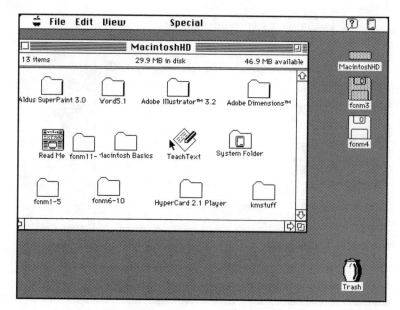

Windows: The Friendly File Manager

The Windows environment is also built on the desktop idea. You've got your traditional icons that open into windows on the screen. When you double-click on a program icon, Windows runs that program.

To create and work with directories (called *group windows*, in Windows), you use the File Manager, a utility that gives you an easy way to see where you are in the thick of things. You start the File Manager from the Main window (double-click the Main icon if you haven't already done so). Then double-click the File Manager icon. When the File Manager starts, you see a diagram of the directories and subdirectories on the current disk on the left side of the screen and a detailed columnar display of the files in that directory on the right (see fig. 19.8).

Adding a Directory

When you want to add a directory from the File Manager, start by displaying the File Manager screen. (No big surprise there.) Then click on the directory (on the left side of the screen) in which you want to create the new directory. For example, if you want to create a directory just off the root, click anywhere on the main bar. If you want to create a subdirectory of FRED, click the FRED directory.

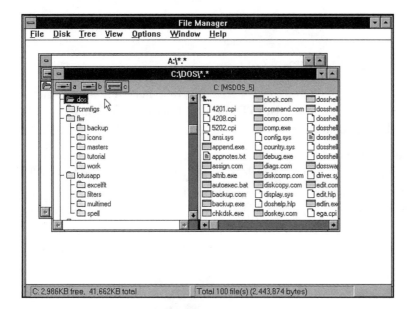

Figure 19.8
The File Manager display.

Next, open the File menu and choose the Create Directory option. A pop-up box appears on the screen, asking you to enter a name for the subdirectory. Enter a name that follows the standard conventions (no punctuation symbols or spaces—something that will help you remember the contents of the directory later. Then click OK.

The File Manager then creates the directory in the directory you'd selected as the current one.

Changing to a Directory

When you want to change to a new directory in Windows, simply click on the directory you want (if you're using the File Manager). The file display on the right side of the screen changes to show the files in the now-current directory.

If you're not using the File Manager and want to change to another directory, you do so by navigating through the various windows on the screen. Double-click on the icon you want to open; the window opens on the screen. You can then double-click on any of those icons to either display another window or run a program. (Similar to the Mac, program icons start programs and group icons open windows.)

Removing a Directory

When you're ready to do away with a directory, first make sure that all the files have been removed. (Similar to DOS, Windows won't let you delete a directory that still contains files.)

Then display the File Manager, click on the directory you want to remove, open the File menu, and choose Delete. When you click OK, Windows will ask whether you want to proceed with the deletion. Click OK again, and the directory is removed.

They're Out To Get Us

So all this seems simple enough. What can happen when you're creating, moving to, or deleting a directory (or folder)? DOS, Windows, and the Finder all let you know when you're treading into dangerous territory. There may be times when you can't delete the directory you want. You might get a message like this:

```
The name "Word5.1" is already taken.

Please use a different name.
```

Hmmmm. . . you can speculate as to what's happened. We've tried to name a folder with a name that had been used. Simple enough.

With DOS, the message might be the following:

```
Invalid directory
```

That doesn't mean that you've got a directory that's no longer valid; it means that you've probably tried to change to a directory and mistyped the name. Check your spelling and try again.

Sometimes, you'll get an `Invalid directory` error when you're simply not far enough down in the directory tree. For example, suppose that you're trying to tell DOS to find a file that is three directories off the root, like this:

```
FRED\ETHEL\LUCY
```

The file you want is in LUCY. You're currently in the root directory (C:\). If you try to change the LUCY by entering

```
CD C:\LUCY
```

DOS is going to say Invalid directory, because there is no subdirectory of the root named LUCY. Be sure to enter all directory names in the path when you are changing, moving to, or deleting directories.

Demon-strations

PC Creation

To create a directory in DOS, do the following:

1. Start at the root directory (\).

2. Type CD, a space, and the name of the directory you want to create.

3. Press Enter.

To create a directory in Windows, do the following:

1. Start Windows by typing *WIN* and pressing Enter.

2. Open the Main group window by double-clicking it.

3. Start the File Manager by double-clicking it.

4. On the left side of the screen, click the directory in which you want to create the subdirectory.

5. Open the File menu.

6. Choose Create Directory.

7. Enter a name for the directory.

8. Click OK.

Mac Style

To create a folder on the Mac, do the following:

1. Open the folder in which you want to create the folder.

2. Open the File menu.

3. Choose New Folder (or press Command-N).

4. Type a unique name for the new folder.

Summary

Setting up and sticking to an organization method for your files and programs is an important part of your computer experience. Keeping things straight is important—especially in those times when you've haphazardly saved an important file somewhere—but *where?*—and you need it desperately. Whether you use DOS, the Finder, or Windows, creating, moving to, and erasing directories is as simple as a two-letter command or a double-click of the mouse.

Exorcises

1. What is the root directory? What symbol is used to name it?

2. What two files are always stored on the root? Why are they important?

3. What analogy is used for the Macintosh environment?

4. Does the File Manager use the same analogy as the Finder? How are they different?

5. Explain the path statement and tell why it is important.

The Healthy Computer: Care and Feeding Tips

Goal

To help you maximize your computer enjoyment (ha) and make your jaunt as a new computer owner less perilous.

What You Will Need

A modest amount of interest.

Terms of Enfearment

mouse pad	toner cartridge
screen saver	burn-in

Briefing

If you follow a few basic rules for the care and feeding of your system, you shouldn't have any of those I-told-you-so breakdowns. Other unforeseen gotcha! breakdowns do occur, however, but regular maintenance and a watchful eye will help anticipate these before they happen.

The System

Talk nice. Nobody likes to be sworn at, and your computer is bound to be more difficult if it is repeatedly the unlikely recipient of your verbal abuse. Remember, the CPU is only as good as the user in front of it.

Don't push the system up against a wall. Literally. The fan needs room to breathe in fresh air (or reasonably fresh), and pushing the system unit up against the wall blocks the air passage, which could result in a meltdown that would curl your hair.

Don't expose the motherboard. Unless you're a certified computer technician (and you wouldn't be reading this book if you were), don't attempt to pop the cover off the system unit and fix anything yourself. This is especially important for Mac users; working on the system unit yourself may void your warranty.

Don't stick foreign objects in the disk drives. Seems pretty obvious, doesn't it? It's the old peas-in-your-ears warning. (Yes, we've been talking to your mother.) But what do you do when you push a disk in the drive, and the label gets caught? Dig it out with a paper clip, right? Wrong. If you can't reach it with your fingers, wait for the computer repairperson to do it for you.

Count to 10 before you start over. If you and your computer are having a power struggle and you need to turn everything off, count to 10 before flipping that power switch back to On. During the shutdown process, give the fan and every other internal thing time to shut down completely before you give it a new power jolt.

The Keyboard

Don't eat and type at the same time. Oh, sure, easy to say—we've all done it. That yeast donut just looks too good to pass up, and you've got to get this report done. . .But your keyboard doesn't like sticky stuff on its keys; it's bound to rebel sooner or later. A key will stick down and refuse to get up. And then another. And another. Better to take a break, eat that donut, and wash your hands instead of mixing business with breakfast.

Be kind to cables. Stretch out if you want to, but don't stretch your keyboard cable to its limit. Long-term stretching can result in a cable that's dying inside. Also, keep an eye out for a cable that's getting itself tied in knots. Keeping the cable straight—but not stretched—will keep your keyboard alive longer.

Keyboard cleaning. Every once in a while, pick your keyboard up, turn it over, and shake it lightly (*really* lightly). Then turn it back over and blow the gunk out from between the keys. You might not see any big chunks of anything, but your keyboard will feel better.

The Mouse

Cool pad, man. Get your mouse a pad of his own, if he doesn't already have one. A mouse pad gives the mouse better traction and helps him live longer. It also helps you be more accurate with the pointer on-screen.

Mouse baths. Depending on how frequently you use your mouse, you may find yourself every other month or so with a skipping mouse pointer. When this happens, remove the mouse ball very carefully and clean inside the mouse with a Q-tip dipped in alcohol. You may want to give your mouse a breathalizer before allowing him to resume normal activity.

A well-connected mouse. Who's to say how it happens? You're using your mouse one minute, and the next. . .it's dead. The pointer just sits there in the center of the screen while you move the mouse around on the desktop. Nothing. Check the mouse connector plugged in to the back of your machine. Chances are, the mouse suddenly loosened itself from the mouse port.

The Monitor

Let it breathe. Again, those little slots along the back, sides, or top of the monitor are important air holes that allow for necessary circulation. All that video circuitry can get pretty warm in there. Make sure that the monitor is away from a wall or shelf so that the air can move around the monitor easily.

Get a knick-knack shelf. Many people put various articles atop their monitor. Monitors generally don't like that. Things fall over, they gather dust, they block necessary air flow. Especially if it's a hairy something—like a cat—get a shelf to store the important somethings you'd otherwise put on the monitor.

Save the screen. Many manufacturers make a program called a screen saver that essentially turns off the display when your computer has gone unused for a certain length of time. This saves energy and also saves your monitor from burn-in; a condition that occurs when a screen that is continually displayed on the monitor gets burned into the screen's phosphor permanently.

The Printer

Let the paper flow freely. Situate your printer in such a way that the paper can move through the printer unrestricted.

If you need to change the ribbon or toner, turn the printer off. This is more for your safety than your printer's. Printers carry quite a bit of current through the various internal parts; toying with things with the power on is inviting fate to step in and curl your hair.

Don't run the ribbon down to nothing. Although it's tempting to leave a ribbon in as long as it's capable of printing an even barely readable character, spend the extra cents and get the ribbon early. Doing so can save some extra wear and tear on the print head.

Recycle your toner cartridges. Many manufacturers now offer reconditioned toner cartridges (kinder to the environment) or reduced rates for cartridges you return yourself. Canon even includes a shipping label with its toners so that you can return your used toner cartridges free of charge.

Disks

No magnets! Remember that anything magnetic—even as small as that little ladybug noteholder—can erase the information stored on a disk. Keep the disks away from anything with a magnetic pull (like your officemate's personality).

Safe storage. Stores sell disk boxes with the express purpose of keeping disks safe from magnetic fields and miscellaneous other dangers. Disk boxes are available for both 5.25-inch and 3.5-inch disks. The investment is small for the return.

Backup, backup, backup. Make copies of all your disks. You may even want to make duplicate copies of really important disks. Then put the originals away in a safe place and work from the backups on a day-to-day basis.

Other Miscellaneous—but Not Worthless—Facts

Remember to give the computer user—that's you—a break. Especially if you're new to computers, you need to stand up and walk around, getting your eyes off the screen, every half hour or so. Computer ailments are becoming increasingly prevalent, and a little prevention could keep you from becoming a statistic.

Invest in some anti-virus software and test all new products. Viruses can wreak havoc on your programs and files. You'll catch them, most likely, from bulletin boards and information services—places where a wide variety of people have the widest access. Anti-virus software is usually pretty cheap and takes just a minute to check a disk—something that may save you weeks of work in the long run.

Always keep a few disks formatted and ready to use. It happens to everyone sooner or later—you're saving a file, when you suddenly get a message that you're out of disk storage space. What can you do? Reach for that formatted floppy. If you don't have a disk formatted, however, you're out of luck: you'll have to exit to the DOS prompt before you can format the disk.

Label your disks. Another major faux pas involves writing over information you really need. A clearly written disk label could prevent that. Take the extra few seconds and write out the contents of the disk on the label (then attach it to the disk). When you change the disk contents, change the label.

Power down in thunderstorms. Listen to your mother—don't make phone calls, don't take a bath, and don't use your computer while there's a severe storm in the area. In fact, unplug everything unpluggable. Better to be safe than fried.

Summary

This encounter rounds out your experience with *Fear Computers No More.* Throughout this book, you've learned to wrestle your fears into submission.

Not so much to be scared of, is there? Your computer is no more than a tool you use to get your job done. Like a stapler, with buttons.

Perhaps it would be asking too much to suggest that you might actually enjoy your computer one day. But it is possible that at some point you'll look around at what you're doing and what you're able to accomplish and think "Hey—this isn't *that* bad!"

Well, maybe.

Key to Success

Oh, shame on you. Cheating. Remember when the substitute teacher in third grade accidentally assigned the wrong math problem—and you found the answers in the back of the book? You were excited (no homework tonight!) and a little worried (what if I get caught?), but worrying about whether or not you were actually learning anything by looking up the answers probably didn't occur to you. (That was part of the lecture your mother gave you later.)

Well, at least you were using your resources.

This appendix lists the answers to those oh-so-difficult problems in the Exorcises section of this book. We hope that you were easily able to find the answers within the body of the chapters, but just in case, we've included them here so you won't lose any sleep.

Chapter 1 Answers

1. Apple.

2. False.

3. The PC was not a friendly machine in that new users felt abandoned at the DOS prompt and weren't sure where to go from there.

4. The Macintosh was the computer "for the rest of us"—those who wanted to use a computer that helped walk them through procedures easily. The Mac uses on-screen pictures, called icons, and the mouse to let users work with programs and data by pointing and clicking—a process much simpler than typing commands on a command line.

5. False. Often the "latest thing" has bugs that have not been worked out. Additionally, the cost is usually higher for newer items.

Chapter 2 Answers

1. b. Spreadsheet.

2. Reusable data. Reusable data. Reusable data. (Error correction and high quality, too.)

3. Organize.

4. False. All kinds of stuff pops up in the business world.

5. Graphics, desktop publishing, project management, and communications.

Chapter 3 Answers

1. False. They are arranged differently and use different terms, but the meat is basically the same.

2. The computer has an 80386 microprocessor that operates at a speed of 25 megahertz.

3. __e__ MHz   a. Memory

   __f__ 512K   b. Device that stores large amounts of programs and data

   __g__ expansion slots   c. 212 million bytes

   __a__ 4M RAM   d. Memory on the video card that speeds up screen display

   __j__ Ultra VGA   e. MegaHertz, which measures the speed of the machine

   __i__ 486   f. 512 thousand bytes

<u> c </u> 212M   g. Room for your system to grow

<u> d </u> video RAM   h. A segment of special high-speed memory that makes processing faster

<u> b </u> hard disk   i. One kind of microprocessor

<u> h </u> 64K cache   j. The current display standard

Chapter 4 Answers

1. Because close scrutiny of badly formed characters over a long period of time will make you grumpy. (And give you headaches.)

2. Mouse or graphics tablet.

3. Because some database files can grow and grow and grow.

4. Oh so true.

5. (1) Read this book (Ha! Forgot that one, didn't you?); (2) Talk to other computer users; and (3) Look through the computer magazines.

Chapter 5 Answers

1. Finding out what you've got.

2. The operating system.

3. c. Turns your commands into instructions the computer understands.

4. (1) Find the person who left it for you and question him thoroughly; (2) Write down all the answers you get; and (3) Have the computer serviced anyway.

5. False.

Chapter 6 Answers

1. False. Computer components are also the big things outside your computer that help it do things beyond its immediate talents (print, plot, scan, etc.).

2. Make sure that all the pieces are there and plan out your work area.

3. (1) Your office space; (2) Available electrical outlets; and (3) Your own comfort (not necessarily in that order).

4. The light direction and type may have a significant effect on your comfort; a behind-your-back window may cause an annoying glare on the screen; too bright lights may leave your laugh lines in a permanent squint.

5. False.

Chapter 7 Answers

1. Tests to make sure that all the computer's internal parts are in working order.

2. The power cords.

3. __c__ Warm boot   a. Powering up

   __a__ Cold boot   b. Techie term for cold boot

   __b__ Bootstrapping   c. Starting over without turning power off

4. False. Get in the habit of backing out of programs using the appropriate commands. When you're back at the system level or the desktop, shut the system down.

5. When you've tried everything you can think of and nothing works. (Or when you see smoke, whichever comes first.)

Chapter 8 Answers

1. Responsiveness is the way in which your keyboard responds to your touch. Highly responsive keys require only a light touch; keyboards with a lower responsiveness require a harder press.

2. The keys were scrunched together, and the Enter key was difficult to hit accurately.

3. The Enter key.

4. Function keys, cursor-movement keys, QWERTY keys, Enter or Return key, and Special keys.

Chapter 9 Answers

1. The Mac.

2. The PS/1.

3. Bus mice and serial (not cereal) mice.

4. Point, click, double-click, drag, and the Bump.

5. Dragging.

Chapter 10 Answers

1. __d__ Computer "brain" a. RAM

   __f__ Room to grow b. ROM

   __a__ Memory c. Motherboard

   __e__ Electric current d. Microprocessor

   __c__ Place CPU is socketed e. Power supply

   __b__ Burned-on instructions f. Expansion slots

2. A BInary digiT, a single pulse of information in a byte (a byte equals eight bits).

3. __5__   Megabyte

   __1__   Bit

   __2__   Nibble

   __6__   Gigabyte

   __3__   Byte

   __4__   Kilobyte

Chapter 11 Answers

1. RAM stores programs and data temporarily, and when power is turned off, the information disappears. Storage keeps programs and data until you erase it; when you start a program, the computer loads the program from storage into RAM.

2. Diskette, hard drive, CD-ROM, and tape drive.

3. You use removeable disks in disk drives and hard disks store much more information than single disks (and can access the information much faster—but that makes three).

4. 5.25-inch __b__ and __d__

   3.5-inch __a__ and __c__

5. They can go south on a moment's notice; they don't like foreign substances like cat hair and spilled coffee.

Chapter 12 Answers

1. Bending over or up to look directly into the monitor is a pain in the neck (literally).

2. The graphics card (also called the graphics adapter).

3. It plugs into a slot in the motherboard.

4. The refresh rate is the rate at which the phosphor gun repaints the screen display.

5. Give it adequate ventilation, make sure that your pets sleep somewhere else, and keep the cords tightened.

Chapter 13 Answers

1. The printer receives data from the CPU, fires up the print head, pushes pins against a printer ribbon, which in turn presses the characters on the page.

2. It prints quickly and is inexpensive.

3. The jaggies are the small visible dots in dot-matrix letters and graphics.

4. The laser printer receives data from the CPU, processes the information, and fires a laser against a rotating mirror that reflects the beam on a magnetically charged drum, which rolls and coats with toner before pressing against the page. (Whew!)

5. PCL and PostScript laser printers.

6. False. (That's an inkjet.)

Chapter 14 Answers

1. From the process it performs: MOdulation DEModulation.

2. Internal and external. Internal modems plug into the motherboard inside the computer; external modems plug into the system unit through an expansion port.

3. Hand-held scanners, half-page scanners, and flat-bed scanners. A flat-bed, because the image doesn't move.

4. Stand-alone faxes and fax boards.

5. You can save the data you receive in electronic form and send computer files easily.

Chapter 15 Answers

1. Applications software are the programs you use to perform specific tasks on your computer; operating system software is the software that makes your computer run.

2. What kind of software do you need now? What might you need in the future? Do you need to be compatible with other computers at home or in the office? How much can you spend? Have you tried the software? And on and on and on...

3. Look for a Help key (usually F1) or a Help command in a menu.

4. Retail and mail-order.

5. Shareware is a try-it-before-you-buy-it type of software; developers ask for a small donation (usually $25 or $50). Freeware is—you guessed it—free.

Chapter 16 Answers

1. That the current directory is the root directory of the hard drive.

2. A portion of the hard disk where you store similar files.

3. The CD, or Change Directory, command.

4. The Program Manager.

5. The desktop.

Chapter 17 Answers

1. (1) Interacts with applications; (2) Takes care of file management functions; and (3) Performs disk management functions.

2. DOS, System 7.0 (Mac), and UNIX.

3. It doesn't control the same functions DOS does; you still need DOS in order to run Windows.

4. False. OS/2 was written for IBM's PS/2 line (and other high-end personal computers, as well).

5. Balloon help, a customizable Apple menu, and multicolored icons.

Chapter 18 Answers

1. FORMAT, COPY, and DIR.

2. __2__ The Mac asks whether you want to initialize the disk.

   __4__ You are asked to name the disk.

   __3__ The Mac tells you disk contents will be erased.

   __1__ You insert the disk.

   __5__ The format is completed.

3. b. Dragging the source disk icon to the target disk icon.

4. True.

5. False.

Chapter 19 Answers

1. The root directory is the main storage area of your hard disk, written as C:\.

2. AUTOEXEC.BAT and CONFIG.SYS. They are used at startup.

3. The desktop.

4. The File Manager and the Finder both use file folders to show directories. However, the overall analogy for the Finder is the desktop, which is not true for the File Manager.

5. The path tells the program where to look (in what directory) for a specific file or program.

Index

E

E-mail, 23
  modems, 187
educational software, 22
EGA, 159
Eject Disk command (Special menu), 241
electron gun, 162, 165
End key, IBM Enhanced Keyboard, 112
energy conservation system shutdown, 97
Enter key, 106-109
erasing
  directories (DOS), 255
  folders (Macintosh), 259
error messages
  Bad command or file name, 218
  Error reading directory, 247
Esc key
  Apple Extended Keyboard, 113
  IBM Enhanced keyboard, 112
Exit command (File menu), 215
Exit Word command (File menu), 212
exiting
  Aldus SuperPaint, 218-220
  Macintosh programs, 216-219
  programs, 97
  Windows Paintbrush, 215-216
expansion slots, 38, 131, 135-136
  hard disks, 148
  motherboard, 133
  mouse, 119
Extended VGA monitor, 39
external hard drives, 148
external modems, 187

F

fan, system maintenance, 268
FAT (file allocation table), 149, 247
faxes, 185, 191-195
  fax boards, 192
  modems, 40
  stand-alone, 192
  troubleshooting, 193
File Manager (Windows)
  adding directories, 260-262
  disk contents display, 245
  disk maintenance, 242-247
  icon, 242
File menu
  Create Directory command, 261
  Exit command, 215
  Exit Word command, 212
  New Folder command, 258
  Open command, 217
    opening Windows Paintbrush, 214
  printing, 180
  Quit command, 218
  Save command, 212, 215
files, 252-262
  AUTOEXEC.BAT, 253
  backups, 96
  CONFIG.SYS, 253
  directories, 252
  document, 257
  Macintosh, opening, 256-259
  modems, transferring, 187
  program, 257
  saving, 96
financial information, 26-27
  see also spreadsheets
Finder, Macintosh operating system, 225-227
fixed disks, 145
  see also hard disks

N